raging for the exit:
a commonplace book

raging for the exit:
a commonplace book

David Breeden &
Steven Schroeder
with
images by
Debby Sou Vai Keng

RESOURCE *Publications* • Eugene, Oregon

RAGING FOR THE EXIT
A Commonplace Book

Copyright © 2012 Steven Schroeder and David Breeden. All rights reserved. Except for brief quotations in critical publications or reviews, no part of this book may be reproduced in any manner without prior written permission from the publisher. Write: Permissions, Wipf and Stock Publishers, 199 W. 8th Ave., Suite 3, Eugene, OR 97401.

Interior and cover images © Debby Sou Vai Keng. Used with permission.

Resource Publications
An Imprint of Wipf and Stock Publishers
199 W. 8th Ave., Suite 3
Eugene, OR 97401

www.wipfandstock.com

ISBN 13: 978-1-62032-207-9

Manufactured in the U.S.A.

Acknowledgments:

Some of the poems included in this collection first appeared online at

http://forgetgutenberg.com/sphericaltabby/
http://revdocdavid.tumblr.com/
in the blog Make No Peace With Oppression at
http://www.wayofoneness.wordpress.com
and on Twitter, @dbreeden.

and, in print, in Steven Schroeder. *Turn*. Virtual Artists Collective, 2012.

Special thanks to Regina Schroeder for inspiration, criticism, advice, and typographic expertise—and to Debby Sou Vai Keng for her paintings, beautiful as always.

...to the circle of friends who make this book a conversation

¶ Inspired by theological commonplace books of the 16th and 17th centuries (before they turned into Protestant dogmatics and systematic theologies) and correspondences in which philosophies and theologies were worked out at the time, we offer this collaboration, back and forth, improvising along the way in two voices that draw on a variety of traditions we find mutually illuminating, a cloud of witnesses. We have been inspired, too, by the poetics of Amos Wilder, Paul Ricoeur, and others identified with the practice of theopoetics and by the critical theory of Theodor Adorno. Presence, divine and human, is connected with language, broadly understood, a rage for order that is at the same time a raid on the articulate. If a *theos* is present, it is *in medias res*, in fragments that defy system. What we have in mind is a theology like music—like language but not language, meaning between, as the broken body of a poem means.

¶ Adorno's 1956 essay, "Music, Language, and Composition," begins with the simple statement that "Music is similar to language." But it continues almost immediately with the equally direct statement that "music is not language." The interplay of similarity and difference transforms both terms. Music, like language, "is a temporal succession of articulated sounds that...say something...But what is said cannot be abstracted from the music; it does not form a system of signs." This leads Adorno to distinguish "signifying language" from "theological" language, of which music, like poetry, is an instance: "What music says is a proposition at once distinct and concealed. Its idea is the form of the name of God. It is demythologized prayer, freed from the magic of making anything happen, the human attempt, futile as always, to name the name itself, not to communicate meanings." This leads Adorno to the question of interpretation, where he makes a key distinction as significant to language as to music: "To interpret language means to understand language; to interpret music means to make music." If to understand music is to make it, then we are on our way to understanding why Marx's philosophy came to focus as it did on production and why *theos* is connected with *poiein* in theopoetics. To interpret the world is to make it, and that makes philosophy more akin to the "theological" language of music than to the "signifying" language of communication. What we are about is naming names.

¶ Clifford Geertz maintains that "The ethnographer… 'inscribes' social discourse"—writes it down—turning it "from a passing event, which exists only in its own moment of occurrence, into an account, which exists in its inscriptions and can be reconsulted." Geertz borrows the idea of "inscription" from Paul Ricoeur who, in asking what writing "fixes," says "not the event of speaking, but the 'said' of speaking, where we understand by the 'said' of speaking that intentional exteriorization constitutive of the aim of discourse thanks to which the *sagen*—the saying—wants to become *Aus-sage*—the enunciation, the enunciated. In short, what we write is the *noema* ['thought,' 'content,' 'gist'] of the speaking. It is the meaning of the speech event, not the event as event." Geertz translates this: "Cultural analysis is (or should be) guessing at meanings, assessing the guesses, and drawing explanatory conclusions from the better guesses, not discovering the Continent of Meaning and mapping out its bodiless landscape." It is not a "discovery" of meaning at all, but a construction (or, as Wagner would say, an "invention"); and, in that sense it is a *making* of world.

¶ To say, as Michael Taussig does, that the storyteller is the symbol of God incarnate is to connect the *wholly* other with an other who is not wholly because she or he is in the flesh and, more importantly, in language. The key is the addition of connection to otherness in the claim that God takes on flesh in the telling (and, symbolically, in the teller) of tales. The tale and the teller bring an audience back home into contact with others who are there only in the teller and the tale. Because the storyteller and the tale are born in migration and return; because migration, return, and staying at home always involve both freedom and coercion; and because God is born in the telling of tales; the birth of God and the origin of language are matters of coercion and freedom—not one after the other, but always both at the same time. That "always both," always reminiscent of *story*, is the real presence of human possibility (which, as Zhao Dongming notes, Ricoeur describes as an "imperative" redescription of reality—and hence the *practice* of ethics), our best hope for cities in which we can not only live but also live good lives.

¶ The practice of theology as we understand it is more like a city than a system. We offer this fragment of collaboration as an instance.

**The Imperative Redescription of Reality
(Or: Occupy a Theonomous Zone)**

The storyteller
and the tale
are born in
migration
and return.

The practice of theology
as we understand it
is more like a city
than a system.

"Music is similar to language."
Began Theodor Adorno, his essay

"Music, Language, and Composition"

(1956). But he continues…
"Music is not language."

The interplay of similarity
and difference transforms
both terms. Music,

like language,

"is a temporal succession
of articulated sounds that…
say something…
But what is said

cannot be abstracted

from the music;
it does not form

a system of signs."

The storyteller
and the tale
are born in
migration
and return.

Adorno distinguishes
"signifying language"
from "theological"

language,
of which music,

like poetry,
is an instance:

"What music says is a proposition
at once distinct and concealed.

Its idea is the form
of the name of God.

It is demythologized prayer,
freed from the magic of making

anything happen,
the human attempt,

futile as always,
to name the name itself,

not to communicate meanings."

Adorno questions interpretation,
his distinction as significant to language

as to music:

"To interpret language means
to understand language;
to interpret music means

to make music."

The storyteller
and the tale
are born in
migration
and return.

If to understand music
is to make it,
then we are on our way
to understanding why
Marx's philosophy focused
on production and why

theos is connected
with poiein in

theopoetics.

To interpret the world
is to make it,
and that makes
philosophy more akin
to the "theological"

language of music

than to the "signifying" language
of communication.

What we are about is naming names.

The storyteller
and the tale
are born in
migration
and return.

Clifford Geertz says,
"The ethnographer…
'inscribes' social discourse"
—writes it down—
turning it "from a passing

event,

which exists only
in its own moment
of occurrence,
into an account,
which exists in its
inscriptions and can

be reconsulted."

Geertz borrows Ricoeur's
idea of "inscription"
asking what writing "fixes,"

says "not the event of speaking,
but the 'said' of speaking,

where we understand
by the 'said' of speaking

that intentional exteriorization

constitutive of the aim
of discourse thanks
to which the sagen

—the saying—wants
to become Aus-sage—
the enunciation,

the enunciated.

What we write is the noema
('thought,' 'content,' 'gist')

of the speaking.

The storyteller
and the tale
are born in
migration
and return.

It is the meaning
of the speech event,
not the event as event."

Geertz translates this:
"Cultural analysis is
(or should be)
guessing at meanings,

assessing the guesses,
and drawing explanatory
conclusions
from the better guesses,

not discovering the

Continent of Meaning

and mapping

its bodiless landscape."

It is not a "discovery"
of meaning at all,
but a construction
(or, as Wagner would say,
an "invention"); and,

it is a making of world.

To say, as Michael Taussig does,
that the storyteller is the symbol

of God incarnate

is to connect the wholly
other with an other
who is not wholly

because she or he is
in the flesh and,
more importantly,

in language.

The storyteller
and the tale
are born in
migration
and return.

The key is the addition

of connection

to otherness

in the claim that God
takes on flesh

in the telling
(and, symbolically,

in the teller)

of tales.

The tale and the teller
bring an audience

back home

into contact with others
who are there only
in the teller and the tale.

Because the storyteller
and the tale
are born in
migration and return;

because migration,
return, and staying
at home always involve
both freedom and coercion;

and because God is
born in the telling
of tales; the birth
of God and the origin

of language are matters
of coercion and freedom

—not one after the other,
but always both

at the same time.

The storyteller
and the tale
are born in
migration
and return.

That "always both,"
always reminiscent
of story, is the real presence

of human possibility

(which, as Zhao Dongming notes,
Ricoeur describes as an
"imperative" redescription
of reality—and hence
the practice of ethics),

our best hope for cities
in which we can not only live
but also live good lives.

The practice of theology
as we understand it
is more like a city
than a system. We offer
this fragment of

collaboration
as an instance.

The storyteller
and the tale
are born in
migration
and return.

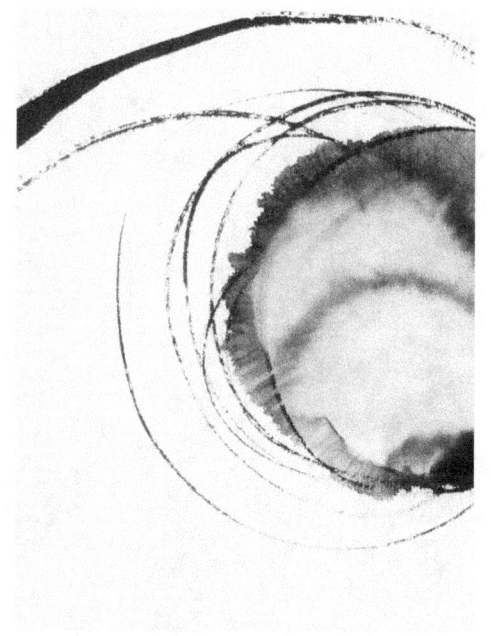

I

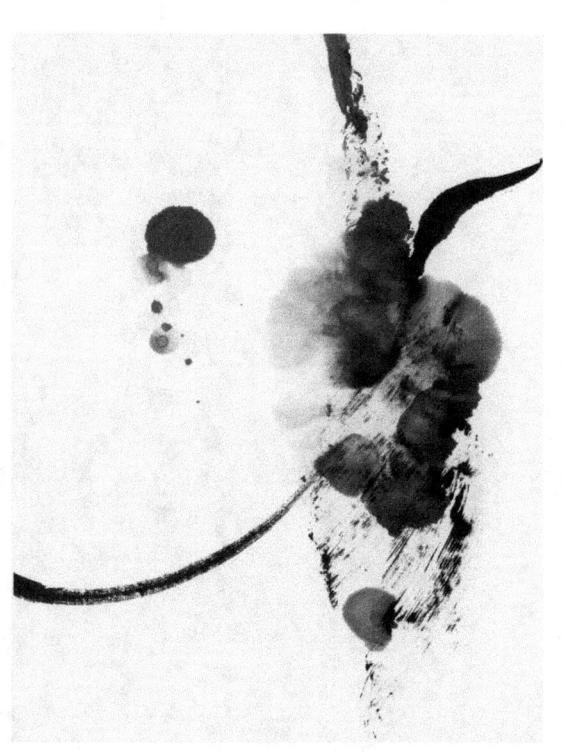

Zoe Aionion

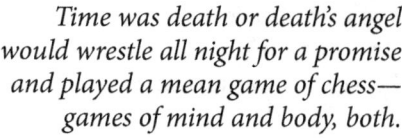

life is short

The Angel of Death
Said to me: "Let me
Lay my cards on

The table—what
You think you know
Is a mistranslation;

Sorry—really we are—
For any trouble that
Might have caused."

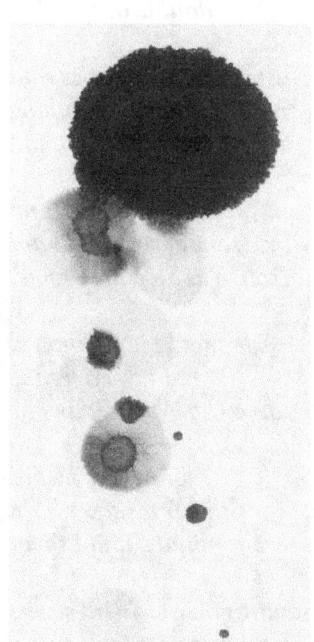

*Time was death or death's angel
would wrestle all night for a promise
and played a mean game of chess—
games of mind and body, both.*

*Now it's poker or penny slots
on the internet. I think I don't know
nothing, and that's no
trouble, but I'd bet*

*the cards had nothing to do
with it. A tortoiseshell
and a fire might do*

*if the arc of the universe
is all you have in mind.*

*But all I know is the arc
is long, life is short,
and I miss Ingmar
every time I see*

*a sign promising me
(as though it would change
the road I'm on) that*

*the loosest slots
are at the next casino.*

At the Wheel

I've seen that road
And that casino
Leering from the desert

And known and
Said to myself
"Some Greek

Must have
Said something
About this

Ages ago
In another
Language and

Another desert
After driving all night
Toward strange gods"

double or nothing

*The last thing Empedocles said
to Aetna was double or nothing
before he crapped out and*

*the damn thing spit up
a bronze sandal cold and hard
for narrative as an empty tomb.*

*He should have known.
I have a feeling
in some Uto-Aztecan tongue*

*loose slots means
there's a sucker born
every minute, and I savor*

*the saving grace of weird sisters
laughing every time a table turns.*

At the Sands

A rockin' guy
Like Sisyphus
Knows each roll
Is rigged and

Every free 'tini
Watered down
Yet remembering

Legends lived
Here once helps
Keep his head
Out of the worn

Carpets and his
Mind off
The 100%

On Practice

That must be
what legends are
for. Kun Iam
can't help

smiling
in the direction
of the Sands when
this thought crosses her mind:

what Li Matou was
selling is not
as far as
one

might think from a casino
modeled on a dream of stars
in a distant desert that has taken
the world by storm.

It's not what goes in your mouth
that defiles you, and she has
seen it all. In this moment
at the bottom of this hill

she is as lucid as Sisyphus while
she plays along with the old saw
everyone knows about
moving a mountain.

Ricci Takes a Taste

Everyone understands
Glitzy after all,
Speaks the language,
And a little guilt,
A little hint of flames
Only makes the glam
That much sweeter.

Eternal payoff—
How's that for bling?
And all you've got
To pay is…

We'll get back
To that—what is
It you call this?

this, that, and the other

*Gilt, you say? Lord knows
it covers a multitude of sins.
Rearrange the furniture,
adjust the lighting,*

*and the cracks are almost all
out of sight. Here this, there that,
this, that, and the other, there's no denying
she's very sparkly—and who's to say*

*what is gold in all this glitter?
Just put your mind at ease
and enjoy the show.*

*We'll worry about the fire
when the time comes.*

A Prayer to Moolah

Moolah is the substance
Of things hoped for,
The gilt on things unseen.

And even though now
We see as through a glass,
Darkly, we know soon
All will appear
In a glossy catalogue.

Thus did Moolah invent cash
And through cash we know
Moolah loves us so long

As we keep His selfishness.

What we see is what
The world is made of

And thus we repeat,
"This is mine and
You can't have it."

> **But about that angel, Zoe**
>
> *I think if I
> heard you
> right you said.*
>
> *About her hand on the table,
> something about a misunderstanding.*
>
> *I suppose we wouldn't know
> heaven if it bit us on the nose,
> and our mind's always
> in some other world
> where* aionion *is*
>
> *concerned, a-bounding
> in metaphysical subtleties,*

lost in theological niceties
where the woods have
no name.

Follow the money they say
like hell I say draw me
she says I know
you're an artist and
you have no idea

why the next thing you say is I
would if I could but I don't do
sketches from memory.

it goes like you without saying
she's standing right there.
And the next thing
you know

you're wandering
around Boston lost
for Christ's sake following

the money. It don't look a thing
like her. It's on its head, man.
Just stand it on its feet.

Like hell, I say.

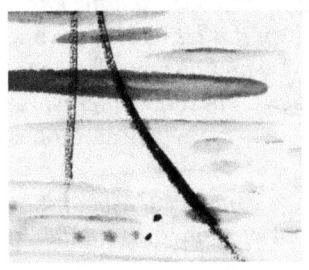

How Many Miles?

Oh, Babylon,
The merchants will weep
And the saints rejoice
When you fall.

Some will get their TARP
And some will cry
And the saints will rejoice
At your fall.

How many miles
To Babylon?

Three-score and ten.

Might I get there
By candlelight?

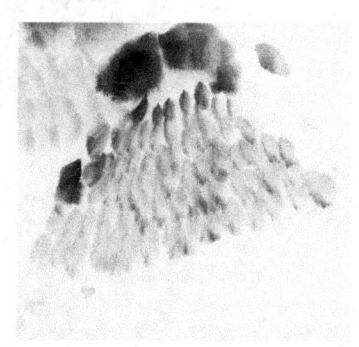

Yes, but you won't
Come back again.

Even if my heels
Be quick and light?

No, there you will find
Dazzling lights and
You will never
Come back again.

Oh, Babylon,
The merchants will weep
And the saints rejoice
When you fall.

But as for the rest

We will have
Forgotten our way
And we won't
Be back again.

there

*we forgot
the song singing
us, thought music
like language ended
when we laid down
our harps and
wept*

*by the rivers
there. We wept,
thinking ourselves
a poem abandoned. When*

*Babylon falls, we will weep again,
knowing every Babylon
that falls is*

*our own Babylon,
every song
outside*

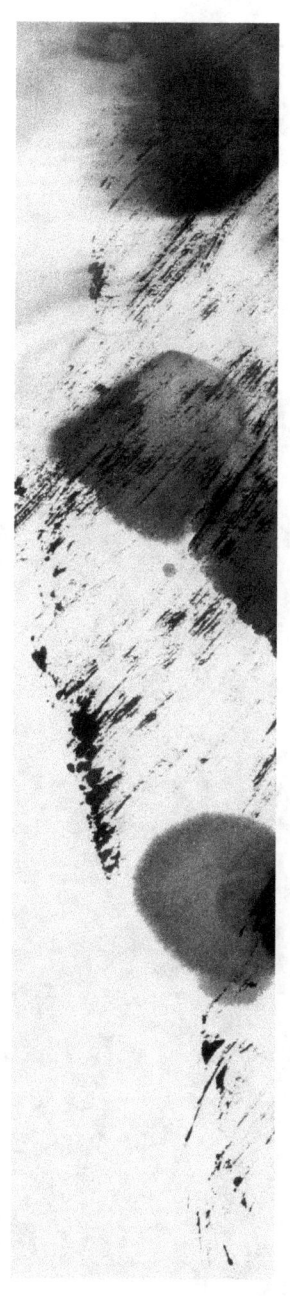

*the city now,
saints forgotten,
clouds of witnesses
falling. Forgive
them. They*

*know exactly
what they
do, and*

*it is never
finished.*

II

The Evil I Would

For the good that I would
I do not; but the evil that
I would not, that I do.
Sure, I want to be keen
On the opposites, really
Really I do. I want to
Work for a Jerusalem,

The new one. And if
The delights, and
The singing all night
Weren't so delightful,
Maybe I would, perhaps
Leave Babylon
In the dust. And I
Might, sometime.
Really, I might.

Yet the good
That I would
I do not;
But the evil
I would not,
That I do.
And so it remains
The invasions,
And the wars, and
Rumors
That drive my will
And it stays

That the good
That I would
I do not; but
The evil I would,
That I do.

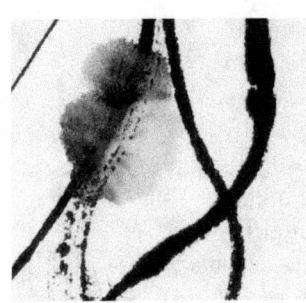

no one is good but

>nothing is
as good as
singing all night

>a little more of that
in our Babylon
and we

>might just
be on our way
to a new Jerusalem

>wei wu wei
a new song singing
that will do

A Musical Interlude to Infinitude

Wu wei,
We know
That time
Is a construct
Of the mind.

Wu wei,
We know
That space
Has been
A pain
To the human
Race.

Wu wei,
Why is it
The Other
Has always
Been such
A bother?

Wu wei,
If we'd
Let those go,
We'd see
The simple
Ebb 'n flow,

Instead we
Wanna know,
Know, know.
Wu wei,
All the fear
Won't take us
Anywhere.

no mind

do not do.
do. not
due.

know? no
mind is a figment
of time's imagination

humans race at
the drop of a hat
no full stop

in that,

and that is
a pain in the ass
to a universe
otherwise
known as
other

wise. time
made up our mind
so everything would happen

(at)

once
on a bet
with space
who never imagined

(that)

Relax 'n
Sing,
Wu wei.

                                 it could—
                                 put space
                                in its place

                                 ,that.

                         more converts
               by half than reason and heart
has reasons reason could not possibly...

                                 you say
                                you've paid
                         your dues? listen.
               you don't know the half of it.
          look here. you ain't seen nothing

                                    yet.

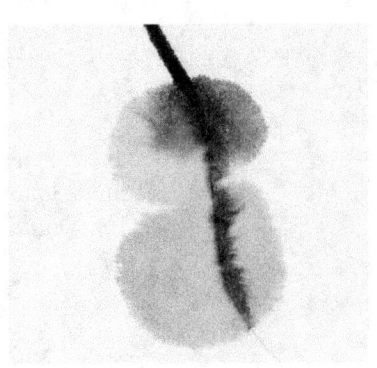

wei

*wu wei
we weigh
our options,*

*but we have none,
and they
wei*

*nothing. do
you see what i'm saying?*

Anecdote of the Words
(apologies to Wallace S.)

I took some words to Tennessee,
And flat they were upon the signs.
Yet the earth bowed to meet them—

No Hunting
For Rent
For Sale
Keep Out!

The hills bowed before them
Everywhere, supine.
And the words were flat
Yet tore the air.

They grasped everywhere,
Splitting rocks into mine
And yours. Spreading boundaries
Everywhere. Like nothing else

In Tennessee.

no apologies

*The thing about signs
in Tennessee is
that they have a way
of making the flat earth happy,*

*and that's when the snakes
come out. People dance with snakes
for the same reason they dance
when some outlaw in
an old Western*

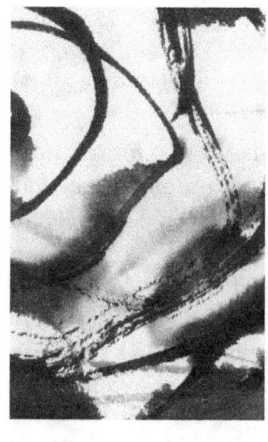

*shoots at their feet
and shouts "dance."*

*They just hope they don't get hit.
They just hope they don't get bit.*

*And that ain't all bad.
If it keeps you on your toes
with hope alive, the spirit might just
take you by surprise.*

*Stopped on the very edge of Nashville once
after driving on thin ice all day
and the people there
told me to be
extra careful when I got to Alabama.
I saw that Saturn towering at a rest stop
outside Huntsville and thought it might be
meant for me, thought they must have been
speaking in tongues, thought "teach,"
said "prophesy!" couldn't keep
my feet from moving.*

*There were crowds in Memphis when
King spoke there for the people
who picked up after the city.*

*Even in the shadow of a goddam missile
on the edge of major weather
on the edge of Tennessee*

*I think it is possible
possible possible.
It must be
possible.*

Driving home from Tuscaloosa
after Bei Dao and breakfast
with my daughter

I have to stop for two days
for a blizzard on this bei dao.
Silent in a dark cloud,

I hear a luminous melody.
Words lie on signs everywhere
like the supreme fiction of an absolute.
If the sound is proper, I cannot say.

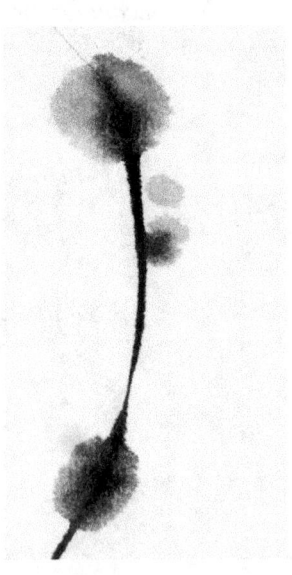

Comfortable Rooms

Ah, we misty poets
Living in the comfort
Of our own minds,
Some in alcohol,
Some in drugs, some
In religion or denial
Bathed. We misty
Poets measuring
Rhythms against
When to say "enough!"
Why is it that no one

Will believe us when
We say this has
Nothing to do with
Politics or empires
Or armies? Nothing
To do with lucre or
Even angels, come
To that—only words
Said in integrity; only
Words said honestly;
Only rhythms said

In a place where nothing
Sobs; where no thing
Suffers. Why can't
Anyone believe these
Misty dwellers in
The chambers of
Their own minds?
All our asking only
For the words beyond
Words, the sounds
Said in integrity?

nothing if not

*a poet in a fog in a town
called black warrior in
the Choctaw tongue*

*is just about right
for politics in these
united states, and I suppose*

*a poet stopped by a blizzard
on the road north is nothing*

*if not misty. Enough
to drive you out of your mind,
where what seems like a scrawny
cry from outside seems to be,*

*sounds to me
like politics,
like a dispersed city,
like a new knowledge of reality.*

Prester John, Esq.

In towns run by poets
There are many
Cockatoos and
Coffee shops and
Ambient noise often

Borders on the spheres,
Or some nosier
Iteration, sometimes
Composed and maybe
Not. After all, when

Hizzoner the Old
Man of the Mountains
Is mayor, nothing
Is true and everything
Permitted, though

Parking is still
A problem. And as
For fire emergencies,
Forgidaboutit! Can
you say "s'mores"?

all true:
how can I keep from singing?

What to do
with that colonial
delusion of a lost tribe
waiting under a presbyter
whose tomb Brezhnev and Monroe
swept every qingming, a spring fashion
that never goes out of style,
the poem of the mind
in the act of finding
an excuse:

*it is necessary necessary
necessary it must be necessary.*

*The best we can do is a city
the people run, poets among us.
And if the time comes to douse a fire,
I'll take my chances with a poet
who's done time watching
on a cold mountain
in a parallel polis,*

*a people with some sense
of how the world does sing.*

Words, Words

"What will it be next?" She asked.
"You know Such things." I looked
At the waxing moon—"Harvest," I said,
Regretting it had to be the obvious one.
"But last month, it was the full Sturgeon,"
I said. And how to work "Full Worm" into
The conversation? When did I become
Someone who knows such things?

Church bells clatter this morning,
Calling the mystic, the bored,
And the poets into the formulations
Each and each set of walls can conjure.
Some crannies will hear, "Father,"
"Kyrie eleison," "Gloria." Some,
"Thank you, Jesus," And, "preach it, now,
Preach it, now!" Some, only silence.

Words do, after all, come too easily,
Sometimes, and others not at all.
And others still, only grasped for
And pasted onto silence just because.
Yet, in beginning and ever the word
Was God; so we must be the proverbs
We wish to say; we must live the wisdom
Life has tattooed into our souls.

this and that

*talk the talk walk
the walk walk
the talk*

*be the word
the way the word*

*was in the beginning
is now and ever
shall be*

*moon waxing waning
this way that*

*everybody knows everybody
means this when they
say that*

*say enough's enough
enough already
every body
knows*

*it goes
without saying
enough said nothing more
stop talking shut the door*

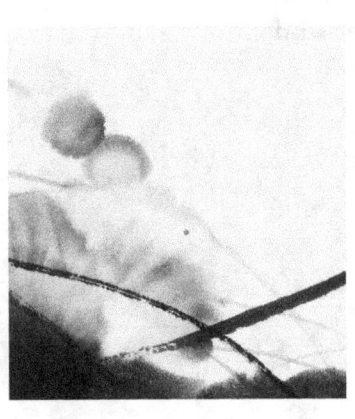

III

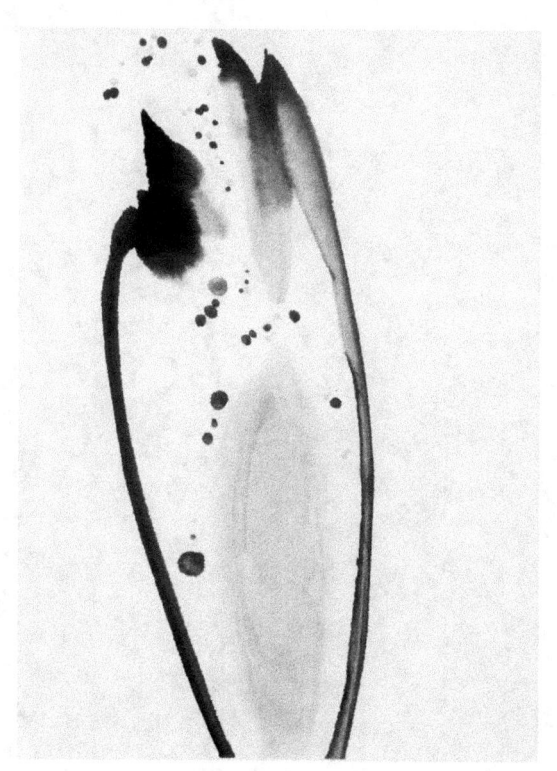

a little meditation on reading Thoreau on writing

*in the middle always present between
eternities past future toeing the line
the arc between death and death
taking place dwelling on it*

*dying to be alive
not in the beginning
the word between this
that and the other beside*

*the point before after
the thing is not the word
but the placing of it always
drawing what is out*

*not to fix the word spoken
before but to dance*

*every word written means
this not that in this
language*

*meaning nothing
totally meaningful you
see what I am not saying
the significance of being not*

*saying who when
as well as what*

*we must be
born again to speak
the language of the written word*

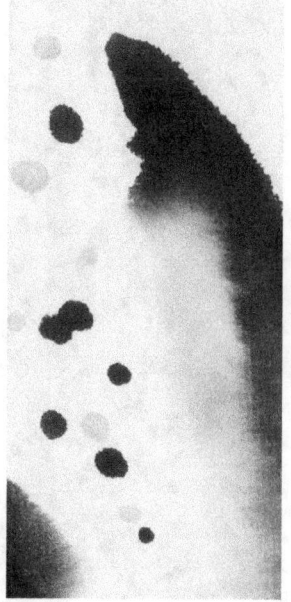

Two Ways of Keeping a Journal

1.

Thoreau sharpened his pencils
Wondering where the words were
That were as fresh as his thought;
Wondering where words were
That another had not claimed.

Couldn't a fresh thought
Find its own body with a whole
Cosmos to write on? Thoreau
sharpened his pencils.
2.

In the beginning was the word,
And Elohim sharpened his wits
With a whole void to write on,
And darkness was upon the deep.
Elohim found words and said,
"Let there be light,"
And there was light.

And Elohim saw the light,
That it was good,
And divided light from darkness,
Calling the light "day"
And the darkness "night,"

Good words for fresh thoughts.

And Elohim said and said,
New thoughts rushing,
New words cast into the deep.

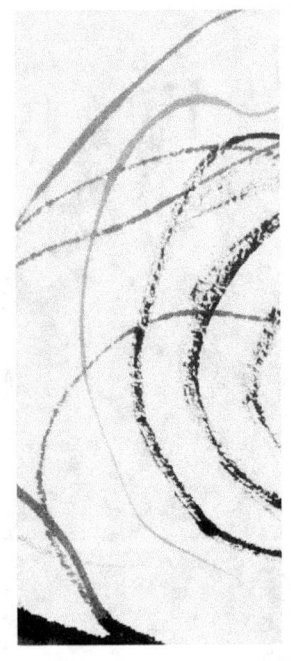

what we mean when we

*Knowing Henry must have made
some of the pencils he sharpened
with wood, plumbago, and a little clay
must have brought a smile to
some of the faces of that strangely
plural god who would stand for
standing for no other.
God knows
making words is making worlds
and making both is a work of the hands—
and that is good, that is very good.*

*A book, a cabin, a place
to dwell. Dust may be such stuff
as stars are made of, but spit on it and it is
still mud until someone breathes the dance into it.*

*Henry must have smiled
at the thought of a god making the wit
he sharpened. He would have none of it,
knowing no time has elapsed
since the corner of the veil
was lifted from the statue
of that god. Time is
not past, present,
or future. It is
in the gap
between the sound
and significance no ear
can hear, language we must be
born again to speak, to hear
eyes open. Let light be,
and we will be
most alone*

*when we go
among others,*

*making god in the image of us,
what we mean when we say we
and make a book of it.*

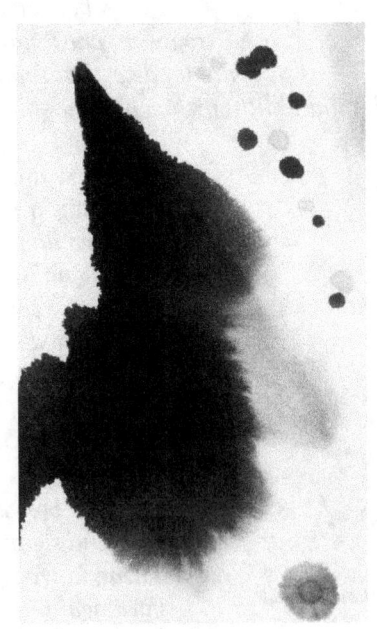

Thoreau Makes his Peace While Jacob Gets a Name

"Henry, have you made your peace
With God?" Aunt Loisa asked
Henry, his lungs filled with lead,
Consumption eating him away.

"I did not know we had ever quarreled,"
Henry said. And perhaps they never did.
Who's to say the Original Screw-Up
Doesn't miss some folks?

"Thank God men cannot fly,
And lay waste the sky
As well as the earth,"
Thoreau said once.

Who is to say that prophets
Don't sometimes get a pass?

After all, when Jacob was alone
He wrestled until daybreak
With a certain man.
When the man saw
That he could not prevail,
He struck Jacob under the thigh
So that Jacob's sinews shook.
The man said, "Let me go,
For the day is breaking."
Jacob said, "I will not let you go
Until you bless me."

The man said, "What is your name?"
"Jacob."
"You shall be called Jacob no more,
But Israel. For you have wrestled with God
And with men and you have prevailed."

Jacob said, "Tell me your name."
"Why do you ask my name?"
He blessed Jacob there. And
Jacob called the name of the place 'Face of El,'
Saying, "For here I have seen God face to face,
Yet I have survived."
So he went over Face of El,
And the sun rose upon him,
And he limped away.

Who's to say
Some of us
Don't get a pass?

"Now comes good sailing,"
Henry said at the last.
Then, "moose." Then, "Indian."

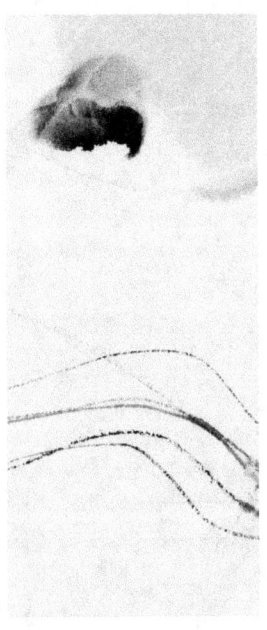

naming names

*What is this thing, I want to know,
with naming names? There is
not one among us who
would not smile*

*at the thought of one some angel
we wrestled all night
once gave us.*

Henry died young, done

*in like every single one of us
(Jacob's god being no exception)
by his work. What we have done to the sky
flying would not, I fear, surprise him.*

*The secret of a long life is knowing
when it's time to go. Remember
the name the angel gave you
and you will and it don't
get any freer than that.*

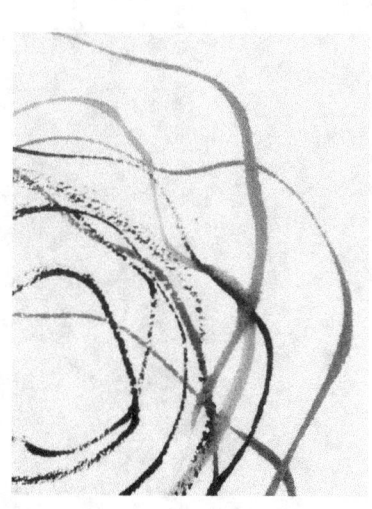

Exodus 3: Punny, Punny YHWH

That YHWH,
Standup,
Saw through the ploy
Moses thought out—

"Uh, when I go
And say God sent me,
They're gonna say,

'What's God's name?'
When that happens,
What am I gonna say?"

So, Yah-Way,
How's that for a pun,
Making up a name
That's a verb—hayah

To be
To become
To exist
To happen

Yes, punny, YHWH,
Saying to Moses,
"I AM THAT I AM.
Say that to Israel:
'I AM sent me.'"

Yes, stammer that out,
Mr. Moses: I am that I am
I am, I am
I will be
What I will be,

Hayah!

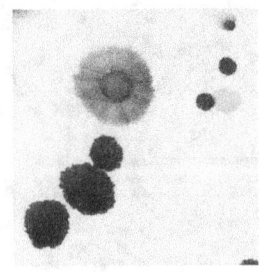

not one

*some kind of poet, not one
to be pinned down,
this plural deity*

*who nouns verbs time and time
again when a prophet lays a hand on him,
sings is you is or is you ain't*

*my baby? nothing to be
done but say
I am, be*

*who you are,
get the joke, but name names,
and answer when a voice
you think you know
cries*

in yet another wilderness

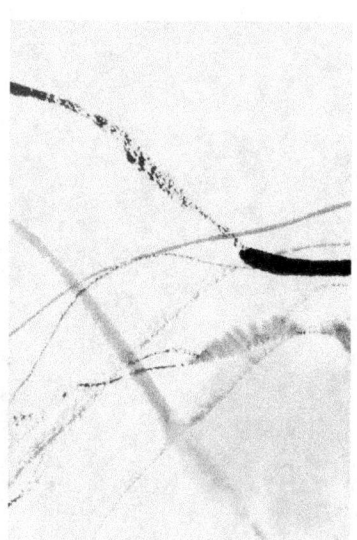

Louis Jordan and the Hydrogen Jukebox

Out in Brinkley, Arkansas
There's still not a lot
To do for anyone but God.
So if you were Louis
Jordon and had a hit song
Percolating in your brain,
And it was 1944,
You would leave too,
And ham it up, "Is you is,"
Black English written
By a Jewish writer.
But what's so new? Besides,
Why not laugh all the way to
Number one on the jukebox?

Alfred North Whitehead
Might have found that
Process interesting, had
He taken time to think
About it. Instead he wrote,
"It is the function of actuality
To characterize the creativity,
And God is the eternal
Primordial character"

By which he meant perhaps
He would leave Brinkley too;
By which he meant…
Something. Something about
Is and ain't and making it so,

Baby.

And Whitehead wrote, "But
There is no meaning to 'creativity'

Apart from its 'creatures,'
And no meaning to 'god'
Apart from 'creativity'
And 'temporal creatures,'
And no meaning to 'temporal
Creatures' apart from 'creativity'
and 'God,'" by which
Whitehead meant something.
Something about
Trusting the process
And picking up the pieces,
Even of crass misunderstanding,
And taking them out
Of Brinkley, Arkansas,
And places like that,
All the way to the jukebox.

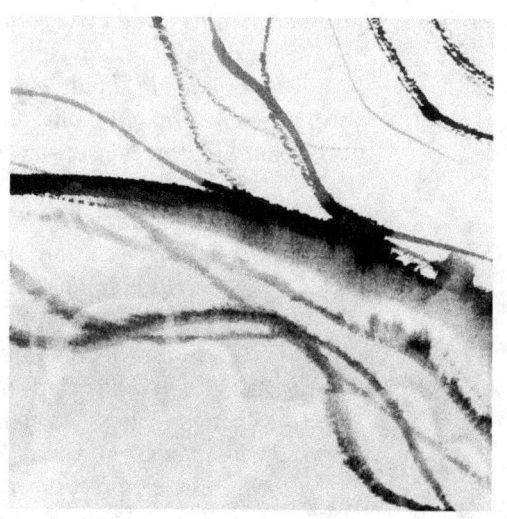

*you know what John Cage
said about recordings in Texas*

I don't know what god does
in Brinkley, Arkansas,
but I know my earliest memories
of miracles are almost all about
waking up in Arkansas
the morning after going to sleep in Texas
when my grandpa and my dad got it in their heads
talking for hours after the kids were all in bed
that it was time right then to take a drive
and visit Grandpa's best friend Clem.

Clem could sing, my mother told me,
like an angel, but he gave it up
when he got religion and
married Lavella.

I never quite understood why you'd give up
singing like an angel when you got religion,
and I know Grandpa's squeezebox
made his house a sanctuary
every time he brought it out after a day
spent building houses—even better
for me when it rained so hard
he stayed home from work and played
in the middle of the day, one more
reason to think rain holy.

Even just taking Mom's word
because Clem didn't sing any more,
I always thought going to sleep in Texas
and waking up in Arkansas must be
what dying and going to heaven
would be like. So I guess
god would feel at home there

*and just hang out. Probably
would have joined us in the stream
looking for chert and stayed
to help pick ticks off later.*

*I'm pretty sure Grandpa never read Whitehead,
though I wouldn't swear to it, because
he always surprised me, and he
knew more than anyone
I have ever known
about concrete
and how easily
it could be misplaced.*

*The first time I read him,
I thought of the hours I spent
at the kitchen table arguing theology
with Grandpa, who was Church of Christ
but never doubted god could take care of himself
so never put up any fences around our conversation.
We'd go on past midnight, then I'd be up when
the light went on at 4 AM for strong coffee
with him before he went off to build
whatever there was to build that day.*

*It's not hard to imagine god a bricklayer in Arkansas
or East Texas, where is you is or is you ain't
was a perfectly plausible way
to pose a question before
someone decided to write it down
and call it dialect. What else would it be?*

*Man, I hope Louis Jordan
got back down to Arkansas
once in a while even after he got famous
so he could make time like god*

*does there as sure as
anywhere.*

*And now you have me thinking of my
great grandpa Heath, who
I never met, so I have to
take my mother's word again.
He was from London, and he used to entertain
her with stories of parallel universes.
Pretended to be deaf and had her wondering
if she was sticking her hand through someone
in another world every time
she reached out to pick a flower.*

*Alfred might have stayed a while if he'd joined us
at the kitchen table some midnight.
We could have had one hell of a time talking
about isness and aintness 'til we saw the light
next morning. And if he'd been there
when I was too young
to stay up that late,
he and Grandpa and my dad
could have piled us all into Grandpa's Packard
and had us in Arkansas by morning.*

*No doubt one god or another
would have been there waiting
with a squeezebox and a song to sing
after morning coffee.*

Surely a Reason

I suppose they could never lose
Their own amazement
At the ground they could cover
V-8 engines on those new highways
Nor could they forget
Their plodding selves
Behind tired horses
Before the war, before the war

And so they drove all night
And told stories of how far
It was they could go in a day
And a night only stopping
Once or twice as if it were
Their duty to embrace
That whole land they'd fought for
In the war

And the places they came from
The farms that raised them
Fell into disuse, mere blips
Glimpsed out other windshields
New cars on new highways
And new thoughts—more, more
Because surely there was a reason
They'd survived the war

I see what you're saying

*Strange turns on every road,
but that old Packard was a straight eight
Grandpa drove until it fell apart.
Dad was the oldest son
in a farm family when farming was essential*

*(as they said), but who knows
what reason?
I assumed then it was
to see a friend, one of those reasons the heart
knows, which still makes sense to me,
and I have to say what the sticker
on the other side of the bumper
from McGovern on my uncle's
truck said when I pulled up to his
Kansas farm a few years later—if you eat
you're involved in agriculture—is still pretty
convincing. But who knows what reason?
I suppose Dad would have said
dumb luck or the grace of God
and hoped there wouldn't be
another one. God knows
people make dumb choices
when they think there surely was
a reason they survived the war du jour.
As far as I can tell, war has nothing to do
with reason and surviving it nothing
more. And those new roads
built later had the next mad war in mind,
speed and redundancy. I've always leaned
to slow and one of a kind,
and to the kind of music
that makes you think
someone who'd drop everything
in a heartbeat to see a friend
might be breathing it, someone
who talks to strangers and remembers
more often than not we have been
strangers and guests, someone
whose heart might be
in the right place to be lifted,
who knows enough about grace to be
willing to be surprised.*

Trust Your…

As usual, he got there
Before me, that darn
Anselm with his "faith
Seeking understanding,"
Or "fides quaerens intellectum"
As he said
In his sassy Latin.
That's what I wasn't seeing
In the clapboard churches
In their de rigueur white
In the faces of anyone
I knew—no quaerens to
Their fides. And no
Intellectum. Nope.
Was it only because
I couldn't feel it?
Was it only because
I could not allow that
Tipping point into
Speaking tongues?
"Trust your instinct
to the end," Ralph
Waldo Emerson said
In his Yankee English,
"Though you can
Render no reason."

Ah. A conundrum for
the intellectum.

Nothing but Middle, Beginning to End

Between Anselm and Saint Ralph, Leonard,
there are always cracks
for light enough
to blind us
while we curse the darkness
on the latest road to our Damascus.

Thank heaven for the cracks,
the cranks, the moments of seeking
something more than craving more on back roads
where the spirit slips into a slow

burn, where locals always speak in tongues.
Trust your instinct to the end. Know
it will go on. No, there is none.

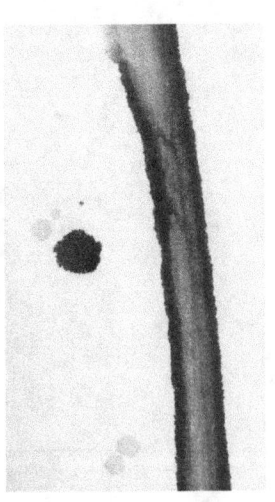

Popeye Takes a Boat

Ham Gravy with his Olive Oil
Has to ask, "Are you a sailor?"
The sort of obvious question
The boss class asked along
About 1929. Repartee.

"Ja tink I'm a cowboy?" Gravy!
Don't give him your boat!

I am that I am,
I ain't that I ain't.
And if you gotta ask
If I can make a rock
So big I cain't pick
It up, you're askin'
The wrong god, bub.

"Ja tink I'm a sailor?
Ask Jonah if you want
To hear fish tales."

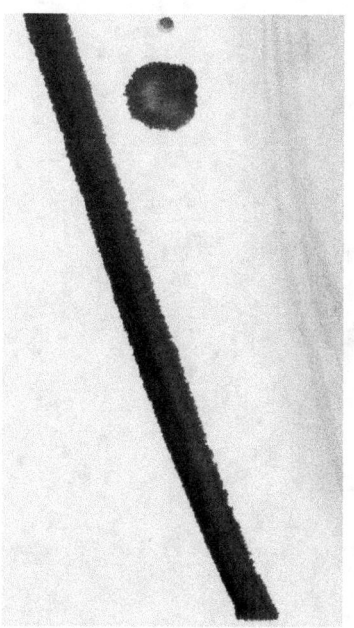

IV

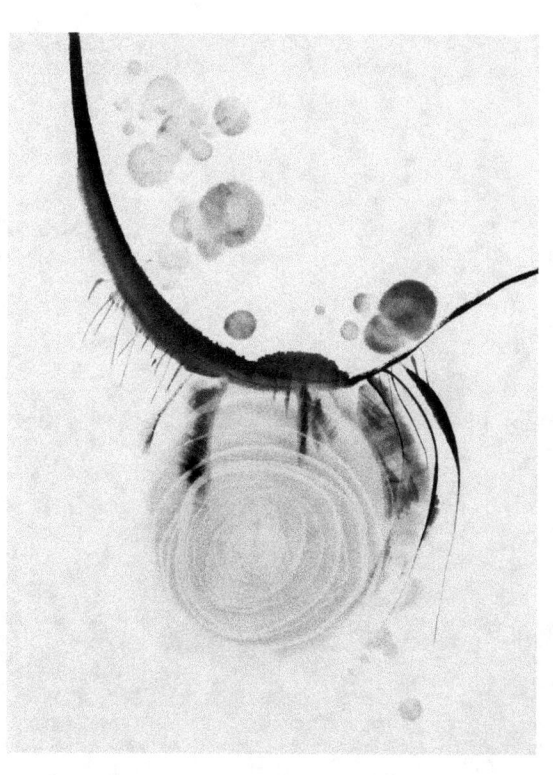

A Tug at Your Sleeve

> *The people kept far off, and Moses drew near to the thick darkness where God was.*
> *Exodus 20:21*

Here is what you
Don't get told:
You must decide.

Yes, must decide
For yourself. Really,
You must decide
For yourself.

If you want God,
There's God.
If you don't want God,
No God.

It's that simple.
It's that complex.

Same reality, different direction.

You can head south—
You can head north—

Up to you.
Down to you.

Different direction; same walk.

Meaning. No meaning.
Walk. Choose.
It's what you
Don't get told:
You must decide.

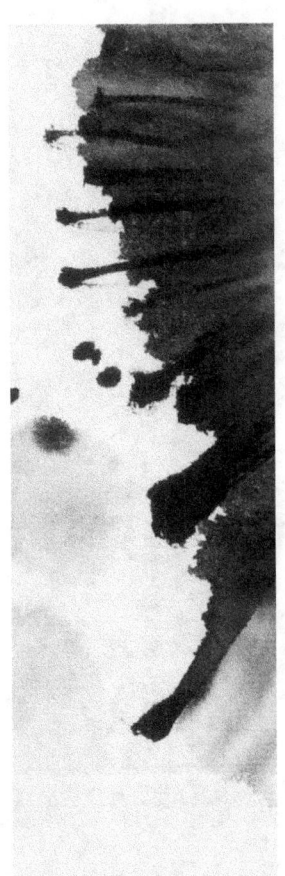

in medias res

the people go without saying
with Moses who is one
of them

what is not said is
that is as it was
in the beginning is
now and ever shall be

world without end what is
not said is god is
the word

in the beginning
where we can
not be

where god can
be nothing

but a word where we are

it's the whirlwind

*there is good reason to stand
some distance from a storm
speaking, cover your ears
when a trumpet blares,
send someone else
to gather words cut in stone
on a smoking mountain,
keep some seconds between
thunder and lightning.*

*it's not what the voice,
some kind of poet, says.
it's the whirlwind.*

*but when every bush is burning
and you inquire after the identity
of the voice that speaks
from fires everywhere so you
can say who sent you, you
will find nothing*

*but "tell them I am,"
which you could
tell them without asking
if you felt the need to tell them.*

*that is no beginning,
but it is the only place
this we can see to begin
in this darkness.*

Good Reason to Stand Some Distance

Brother Ike claimed he was raised
By cannibals. "Yeah, I ate people,"
He'd say, as he pranced on the altar rails
At revivals when I was a kid. "But
The Lord done took that desire away!
He done took away that perversity,
Cleansed me white as the driven snow!
And now I am a headhunter for Him!"

"Oh, sweet, sweet Jesus! I 'go forth
As brightness,' and 'thy salvation is
As a lamp that burneth!'" Brother Ike,
After he'd preached for hours, after
The altar call, would mop his brow
And offer to show us kids his teeth,
That had been filed, he claimed, to
Razor sharp. Nobody was so brave.

"'Truly in vain is salvation hoped for,'"
Brother Ike would sweat and pace,
"'From the hills,' or money or job!
'Nor from the multitude of mountains!'
Yea, not in the rainforest neither!
'Truly—only—in the Lord Christ our God,'
Yes, sweet Jesus! Is the salvation of Israel.'
Truly now I'm a headhunter for the Lord!"

keep on turning

*Brother Ike and that talking whirlwind
have me thinking about the old sharecropper
in the Grapes of Wrath who knew the difference
between a storm and a bad thing made by men—
the possibility of change, more or less,
which is just about where the gospel begins
if I read it right. Not a bad idea
to keep your distance
from both until you have some sense
of what you can do about it—
and take a long hard look
at any Moses who walks right in
as if he and god were drinking buddies,
as if he's going to have a little sitdown
and march right back out
with an answer cut in stone.
The sharecropper wouldn't much mind
if you wanted to pray for rain
(he'd probably pray with you),
but what he had in mind
was changing the way you drive
the tractor and doing something
about the predatory financial system.
When our Lord Jesus Christ, you might say,
called us to repentance, he meant our whole life
should be repentance. Not some magic coin
flipped into a tin cup or a pork barrel
in passing so another soul would fly.*

*But listen with your heart, child,
while we open a school for God's service.
There are four kinds of soldiers
in the army of the Lord,
and god knows I'm willing to give
most of them the benefit of the doubt.*

*Their hearts are in the right place.
But with some you need to keep
an eye on the exit and
a hand on your wallet and take
every promise with a grain of salt,
especially where diamonds are involved
and they say god wants you to be rich.*

*There are those waging their war
under a rule and an abbot. You will
find them at the downtown Baptist Church
Sunday mornings and Wednesday nights
and at the stadium in time for kickoff on Friday.
They call their abbot doctor, and he and they
are pillars of the community.*

*There are those who have been around a long time
and don't get around much any more.
They keep to themselves,
listen to sermons on the tv,
read the Bible every day, look
forward to days the pastor calls, and
know the day is coming when
Jesus will call them home.*

*And then there are those who are
unchurched, the worst. They
call holy what they like.
What they don't they call unacceptable.
They may dress up and drop in to a ceremony
on Easter, but you will know them by
the blank look when you say
john three sixteen or ask if they
know Jesus as their own personal savior.
Pray for them.*

*And there are the gyratory,
worse than the worst, who wander,
restless servants to the seduction
of their own will and appetites.*

*It's all about turning, see. Those gyrations are
tricky, and (if I recall my Levi-Strauss right)
the first kind is cooking for Brother Ike,
who has been born again
as a politician.*

Hap and Humility

Brother Hap learned
How to play dead
At an early age,
After the National Guard

Thought they'd killed him.
A little purge of mine workers.
It left him humble somehow.
Not the usual Pentecostal—

"I ain't sinless," he'd
Say, "I just sin less."
And, "You don't know Jesus
Is all there is until Jesus

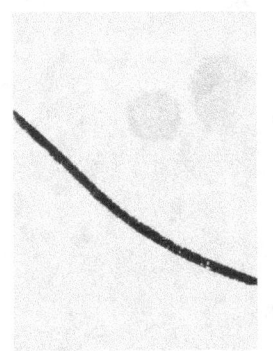

Is all you've got!" He'd
Look over the pulpit
Nearly as tall as he was
And say, "Now, brothers

And sister, I'm a-gonna
Tell ya one on myself!"
Then off he would go
Into the stories that

Made him. That taught
The Christian way even
Though in his later years
He drove a Cadillac.

"Sisters and brothers, I'm
A-gonna tell one on myself—
I was out a-shoppin'
Just the other day…"

Dying to be the Way

For a story formed people,
it's a world of words
to the end of it—
and what people isn't?

If there is a Christian way,
it's telling stories on yourself, though
I'm pretty sure the one that can
be told is not the only one.

But I'm here to tell you
I can't tell you anything else
unless you can hear what
I'm not saying

better than I. It's every breath
you take, more or less, more
than the way you're on or
what you're driving or

what is driving you on. Even in the Caddy,
your other vehicle is the music of the universe
reminding you that sin less means no
more than sinless when

missing the mark is missing the mark
and the mark don't mean nothing, more
or less, unless it is some story you
tell on yourself when God says

in ten words, "be holy." Learning to play
dead is learning to die, and,
take my word, there is no
end to that, Hap,

*as long as you are living. Odd
to think of a usual Pentecostal when
there is no Pentecost that is
usual with all that wind*

*and wandering. Walking through
the Union Miner's Cemetery
in Mount Olive, I've stopped to think
of Mother Jones there praying for the dead.*

*Miners know a thing or two
about spirit after breathing coal dust
for a lifetime. Unusual
Pentecostals,*

*they're still, playing dead all these years
later—and there's nothing to be done
but fight like hell, pray for the living,
play dead learning to die dying.*

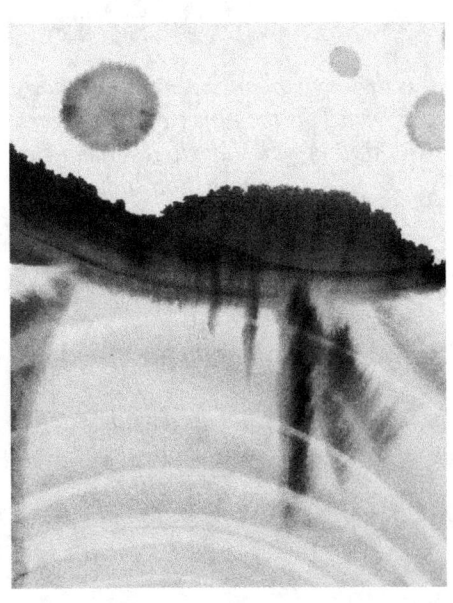

Logos in the Mythos

Somebody who somewhere
Has "postmodern" in
The resume tells me

The meta in the narrative
Is busted like a wagon
Wheel headed for 1914.

Where does that leave
The Christian story
That has so little story

And so much old Greek
Abstract? And all those
Hebrew yarns—you know

The ones turned to
Abstraction on a Christian
Thread too? Oh, yes,

You put the logos
In the bios
And you mix it all up

You put the logos
In the mythos
And you mix it all up

You put the logos
In the bios
And you call me

In the morning.

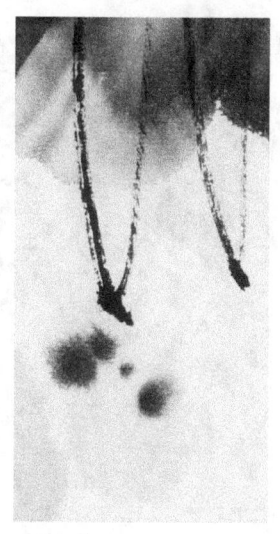

Nomads, not Monads

*Scattered from here to tomorrow
full of possibility, more stories
than Coyote and a fallen
star. No better place
than the depth of darkness
radiant to call a psalm, call a psalm
again when morning has broken,
always first, nothing moving
but a mountain, still under
the eye of a blackbird naming
names, singing songs of songs,
telling stories of stories, holies of holies,
alephs to omegas. Break a meta here
and there for the light, for the light, always
another. Kurt says it's turtles all the way
down, meta turtles up beyond words
to silence, no formal system final,
nothing to do but rise, take up
your house, and walk.*

Primacy

Who really was it first said, "All is one"?
Someone in the oldest profession,
Realizing the contours of her future?
A soldier in some foreign place again dying for…
A mother, her child dead?
Who was it first thought, "All is one"?
Not a priest headed for the front, covering his butt.
Not a philosopher with a party to go to.
Not a king with his power in multiplication.
Who was it first said, "All is one"?
No doubt one of the silent ones, stunned
Into staring at the sky.
"All is one. Damn it all. All is one. I can go on."

one two three

One of the silent ones walking walked that line
years before Parmenides, proving Zeno
wrong before he was born. But
that didn't stop him. Always
in the wrong, Søren said,
and it's one two three

what are we dying for? Damn I can
go on is one step more after
don't mean nothin'

and there may be
something to be
said for that

Once in the French Quarter

Once seven men went out
To take seven pictures
Of people taking pictures.

All seven came back believing
They had found a key to
Perceiving as they had not seen

Before. All seven came back
Convinced that art is not
In the eye of the beholder.

Imperialistic War is a Rebellion of Technology

"Fascism sees its salvation in giving these masses not their right, but instead a chance to express themselves."
—Walter Benjamin

A story of seven people
taking seven pictures
of (seven?) people
taking pictures

once in the French Quarter
seems to solicit some sort of numerology—so,

a sketch. If seven people taking pictures

*were taken seven times by seven
people taking pictures, that is
seven to the power of three,*

*and the trinitarian implications of a holy number
to the third power seem so self-evident
as to go without saying.*

*If not, still, the seven
people came back convinced,
and that would be the third
seven (and, if not,
a fourth,*

*which would be a holy number
times itself another holy
number of times).*

*But I digress, and, even
numerologically speaking,
multiplication is never in the I
of a beholder. And where does that leave art?*

*As it happens, I say art is not except as it happens,
which would mean the seven men taking seven
pictures would be right. And, by George,
I think, therefore, esse est percipi,
or some such thing.*

*Someone seeing the photos is sure to ask, "But
is it art?" And knowing how one thing
leads to another, someone*

*might find his way from there to thinking
of arcades and add "in an age of
mechanical reproduction."*

*Reception in a state of distraction...
profound changes
in apperception...
symptomatic of perceiving
as they had not seen. They say*

*Fiat ars—pereat mundus. And they
do go on and on, in saecula saeculorum,
dropping their states of distraction everywhere
like bombs, until the whole world is laughing,
until it forgets it is laughing at itself.*

The other day I buried a man

Who'd had a good life except
His father had hanged himself
Not enough time after
Fighting the Nazis.

Perhaps there's never enough
Time, but 1947 was soon.
And the man I buried was left,
Four years old, to wonder why.

When he told me the story
Of a Norwegian minister
Who went back to fight
I thought that made sense.
When he told me his dad's
Hero was Kierkegaard,
I said, "Norwegians should
Never read Kierkegaard!"
And I didn't know
If I was joking—Either/Or
In a time like that…
At a time when certain masses
Were expressing themselves…

But I suppose his dad went
Into the technology of war
Seeing "it all perfectly;
There are two possible situations—
One can either do this or that.
My honest opinion
And my friendly advice is this:
Do it or do not do it—
You will regret both."

Yes, Søren, that about sums it up—
Sometimes, all the way
To the end of a rope.

wei wu wei: always all the way to the end of a rope

>Call no man happy, more than one
>old Greek said, until he is dead.

>And I still hear choirs singing can't no one
>know at sunrise how this day is going
>to end. Can't no one know

>at sunset how the next day
>will begin. You'd think that long
>dark night of the soul would be a poem

>to write in northern light. But the kind of poet who
>listens in this cold light learns what passes
>for dark night is all the light

>there is. We may be flames pouring out of the earth,
>but in this twilight where all cats are gray,
>undiverted by the cat we love,
>we can become all ears
>for one word.
>The measure of a man is how far it is
>from what he understands
>to what he does.

>Do not do. Work
>is love made visible.

God's Gonna Cut You Down

"You're born but
You ain't dead,"
My gramma
Used to say
When she heard
Someone say
Something she
Thought full
Of human ego.

When she
Said she'd do
Something, she
Always said,
"Lord willin' 'n'
The creeks don't
Rise." Same
Thing—a bow
To God's Will,

Inscrutable,
Our puling
Little selves
Like sheep,
Like babies.
Want. Want.
"It's God's will"
Stopped any
Argument.

"Good Lord'll
Take you down
A peg. You're
Born but
You ain't dead.

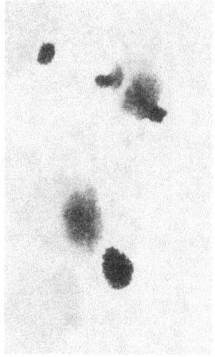

Flit around
With butterflies,
You end up
In a cow pile."

Ego

*I learned it was time to be still
when Granny said "Don't be ugly,
be sweet"—and wise to be
as sweet as I could a while,*

*lay low, and wait for her to settle
into her afternoon stories.
I don't recall her ever calling
on god to settle an argument,*

*god bless her. I suppose
she'd had too much up close
experience with tornadoes
to risk calling down a power known*

*to speak from whirlwinds on
matters of theological significance
(and what matter isn't?). God knows
an argument could get ugly,*

*but years of watching what took place
between Granny and Grandpa taught me
it could also be a way of making
love—and there is nothing*

*sweeter. Cricks were mostly empty
things most of my life, and Granny
was a force of nature. So when
she said she would*

*and added that old saw
with a twinkle in her eye,
I was pretty sure god would
stay out of her way and not be*

*ugly. Granny wasn't big
on talking religion. (That was
a game I played with Grandpa
at the kitchen table, where*

*no transubstantiation
was necessary to know god
present, body and soul, in
coffee and cold biscuits,*

*and the sanctus bell was
laughter.) Her theology
was a work of the hands
in her half acre of flower beds.*

*I took it in through fingers and toes
between moments of worship when
the whole thing bloomed.
She was Baptist, but*

*I studied smells and bells
with her a long time before
I swung a thurible among
Anglicans in a high church.*

*Flitting with butterflies was a good thing,
even if it meant a lot of shit (which
Granny could hear as well as god
at every turn in those tischreden
with Grandpa, full of it). Most of the time,
she thanked the lord for bullshit, turned it
with hands and spade into dirt that wasn't
much good for growing things without a bit of it.*

Uncle Woody Zen

My Uncle Woody was the last man
In the county working oxen.
People would stop their cars by
Just to watch. And it was quite
A show—"big" and "dumb"
Both do describe oxen well.
He used a long pole to drive them.

First is knowing the ox is gone.
This my uncle never learned;
Nor did he trust shoes, come to that.
Then comes the search.
And my uncle never did that either.
He'd come full circle
Without ever leaving
Home. We took him to the doctor once
Thinking it was brain cancer,
But it was only wheat
Sprouting in the dirt in his ear.

Uncle Woody drove his oxen
Nearly to the Twenty-First Century,
Never realizing that
The ox had gone;
Never missing the rose,
Or the snows of yesteryear
That others of us find must be
Placed in a set, symbolized
In naming—"The ox is gone."
"The rose is faded."
"Where are the snows of yesteryear?"
My uncle circled in the round ditch
Worn by his oxen, 'round and 'round.
He never knew they had gone.

Program or Be Programmed

*I've seen an ox working a plot on a mountain
in Tibet where a tractor could not go
and a farmer's feet could not be
trusted alone on the slope
with a machine.*

*When agribusiness reaches him, the farmer
and the ox may be gone—the plot too,
unless they move the mountain.*

*First is knowing the ox, who was
there before the man who may
not know himself mistook
him for a tool.*

*Second is knowing the tool,
how and when to use it,
when it is using you.*

*It's not tools true prophets rail against but
users standing on their heads used by them.*

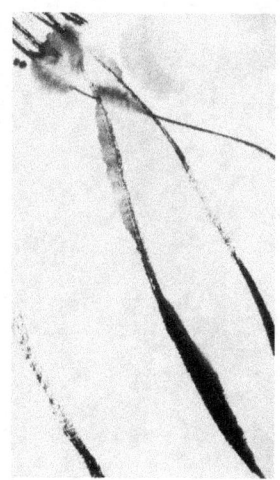

*And it takes a poet
with a good command of tools
to remember what was sprouting
from the dirt in an uncle's ear, to sing
it with a faded rose, a gone ox,
and the snows of yesterday.*

Interfaith Action, Capitol Steps

Yesterday I sat for three hours
In the boiling sun on the capitol steps,
Me in my priest's collar and he
In his—whatchacallit—Buddhist robe,
The same colors as the Dalai Lama.
We were there on September Eleventh
To show what interfaith looks like.
And it looked like crimson and gold
And all black and a lot of sweat, the
Tibetan Priest and I broiling in the sun.

And

We may have been showing interfaith
At work, but mostly I cooked in my
Western grease, late middle-aged and
Swilling bottled water. But he, eighty
If he was a day, sat, unmoved. Quiet.
Unruffled and unsweating. Eighty if
He was a day. And my first impulse
Was to ask afterwards, "How did you
Do that?" But I know how meaningless
The question is. The mountain climber

Nagarjuna already said a thing or three
About it—Whoever sees that all things
Are connected understands suffering,
Its cause, its ceasing, and the path away.
Oh, and, incidentally, how not to sweat,
Or how to sit still and watch it pass.

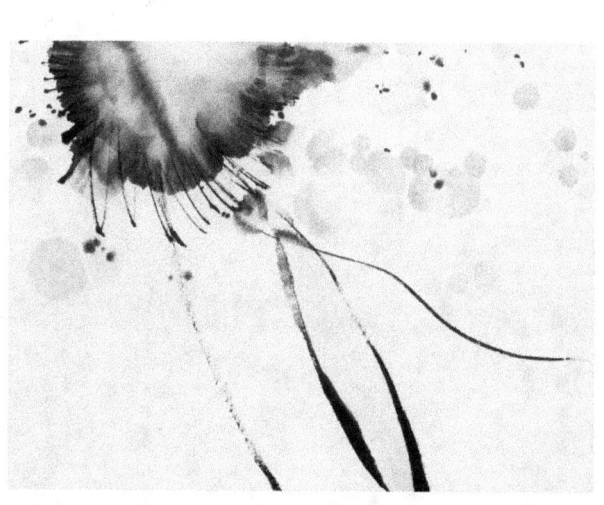

V

Trumpets and Thunder on Horeb

The people stood
Afar off, and Moses
Drew near to
The thick darkness
Where God was.

There the LORD said
Unto Moses, "You shall
Have no other gods
Before me." And
There the LORD said
Unto Buddha, "Mind
Precedes all mental
States." And there
The LORD unto Francis
Bacon, "Knowledge
Itself is power." And

The LORD said unto
Them, "Go down
At once! Your people
Are acting perversely."

wei wu wei

*Seeing that the people
had gotten down,
the LORD said
"get down with your people."*

*Buddha said, "no
matter, never mind,"
plucked a flower.*

*Francis said, "I'm down
with that," took the flower,
tortured her for secrets.*

*Moses went down,
said "go." Laozi,
on his way,*

*turned
to Zhuangzi without
a word. Zhuangzi said*

*"That dark, dark radiance.
Don't it make you wanna dance?"*

*Krishna was,
with a circle of Gopis,
while Jesus looked to see
where the good wine was stashed.*

*The LORD laughed, said good,
very good, and took a little break.*

Further Lessons from Cana

"Imagine," he said, "a groom and his friends.
Who is going to fast before the big day?
Nobody. Someday, the groom will be gone.

Then, they can fast. Look at it this way:
No one sews a new piece of cloth,
One that hasn't been shrunk,

onto an old garment
(except maybe in a sweatshop!),
because the new piece will tear away

and make matters worse.
Or look at it this way:
No one puts new wine into old wineskins

(Except maybe Four Buck Chuck).
That just busts the old skins and spills the wine.
New wine, new wineskins.

And as for boxed wine,
Don't get me started!"

let the people say

*Jesus, Li Bai, bring on the wine,
tip your golden cup full to the full moon
now, and let all the people say amen.*

First Alto

St Francis taught frogs
To sing the praises

Of God; He taught
The sheep to baa

Their own hymn.
Everything, he said

To every one, has
A hymn to sing.

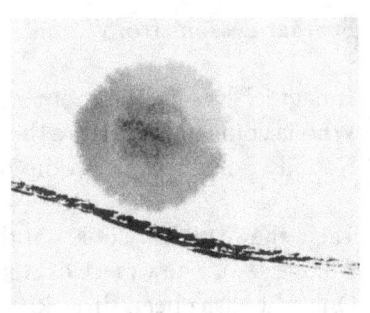

For All the Saints

*The frogs thought Francis droll,
sang with their little brother
so, singing, he could learn to sing
praises he had not yet thought to teach.*

*The sheep practiced the simplicity
they preached, and Francis
never doubted they were
holy as brother sun*

*or sister moon, who
kicked off her shoes to dance
on the water floating Li Bai's boat,
discalced before Teresa or San Juan*

*in una noche oscura, never
lost in a cloud of witnesses,
a community of saints, minding
Bonaventure's journey, knowing*

nobody went nowhere they were not already.

Sheep People

What's the deal with shepherds?
Moses is one; David is one;
Jesus plays one in metaphor,
I suppose because he didn't
Have the bucks in real life.

But wait, Moses worked for
His father-in-law; David for
His daddy; and Jesus…
Well, his paternity is still…
Debated…What's the deal

With sheep? I learned to
Shear them for pocket money
When I was a kid. I learned
To dock their tails—a nice
Way to describe a hammer,
A post, and a big knife.

I learned that they are
Stupid, stupid animals,
Baaing madly after the rest,
Feeling lost, when if only
They had turned around…
Stupid animals. Baaing
With their attitudes right
Up to that big knife to
The throat. And the smell…

Moses got out of the business
When a job like Leader of the
People came along. And David
Grew out of it, though
He sure rubs our nose in
His peasant past. No,

Francis was a saint for
Teaching them to sing. And

Jesus. Well, my kind
Of Shepherd—talking
About it while there's not
a hint of manure in sight.

Simple Gifts

*No argument here about the sainthood of Francis or
the simplicity of sheep. Shearing sheep was a
seditious act where I grew up, indelibly
connected with herding them, but I confess
I spent enough time in their vicinity
to seriously contemplate the possibility
that they could be classified as vegetables
when a friend tempted me with gyros not long
after I gave up meat. Jesus, a carpenter who learned
the trade from the saint who married
his sainted mother knew his audience
well enough to know he had to know
something of the dimness of sheep so the shepherds
in the crowd could nudge their neighbors and tell
them what it really meant to leave ninety-nine
alone and search for one. The faith wasn't
in the ninety-nine or the one simple
soul lost, so the shepherds could
think themselves saints for putting up with
the simple-minded creatures. And Francis would
smile and nod and go on singing with them.
If anyone said anything about blindly
marching after the one in front,*

*feeling lost, I think Francis would still
sing, not much interested in the sainthood thing
but certain sainthood, if it was anything at all,
was a gift god would bestow on all god's
creatures, considering the lilies, sure as rain,
and Jesus would say "let he who is without sin…"
and leave out the part about the stone knowing
where humans were involved a hail of them
would follow. God knows no one
would breathe a word about the sewer
but, on that count, even the peasants of Palestine
could ponder a good word in their hearts
for Roman engineering.*

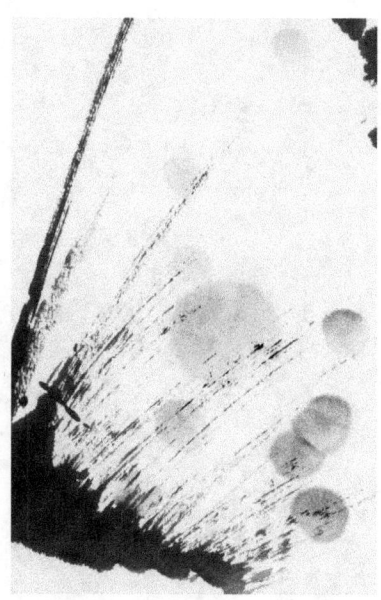

As Larks, Harmoniously

'Tis a gift to be simple,
But to be kind
Is a pain in the ass
Most of the time.
Oh, all we sweethearts
Hovering over abysses
Of our own conjuring,
The sorts of places only
Twisted twits could
Construct in
The convolutions
Of our own egos.

With brains like ours
It takes stripping in court
And leaving town butt naked;
It takes rebuilding
Ruined chapels;
It takes hugging lepers
And singing with
Flora and fauna
To clear just a little path,
Tentative at best,
A little dodge to fool
The mind to forget.

It's a gift, simplicity;
A white elephant or
Elephant in the room.
It's a gift, kindness.
that cost only everything.
Entirely unlikely. OK,

A miracle.

yes, a miracle

No either or, this.
Love kindness do justice
walk humbly with god, simple as that.

Be kind, dammit.
A pain in the ass, no doubt.
Didn't Balaam's have a thing or two to say

about that? And god made
a gourd to demonstrate
for Jonah when he

turned and ran because (being a prophet after
all) he knew his god, thinking of cattle in
Nineveh, would repent

and make a fool of him. Turn
and turn and turn until you know
you can't give what you don't own

and you don't own nothing. Brother
Martin simply gave his cloak
to a stranger, put down

his sword, put down
his power (and C.T. stood
unmoved while some redneck

broke his jaw) because it
was not lawful for him to do
otherwise. Simple, not easy.

But right in that now,
one moment in
a whole life

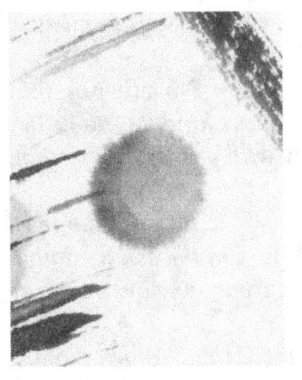

*turning. Brother
Francis and Sister Clare
embraced lepers with a kiss*

*because they were sisters
and brothers, strangers
and guests, and they*

*knew enough to know
this, too, is part of the dance.
What you do to the least, as I recall,*

*The least we can do. It's that other brother
Francis clearing paths that has
me concerned.*

*the one whose children
always seem to have a mandate
from one United or another to protect*

*civilian lives. Nature's secrets are common,
and only a fool working 24/7
to be a saint by being*

*right would torture
for them. It is true that
as a rule, every poet is a fool—*

*or so they say, which makes us
cousins of Francis and Francis, I suppose
casting about for secrets, casting stones, certain*

*we know which chapels to repair, which sacred
ash to sweep away. Certain we know a war
of necessity when we see one.*

Guna / No Guna

Ramakrishna started out dual
In a little temple to Kali.
Before an Advaita Vedantin
Came along saying, "You
Can't get all the way with that!"
So Ramakrishna sliced
Kali in half and walked
On the Ganges as many have,
Saying, "Sure God manifests;
Why would that matter?"
Then he gave Christianity
A whirl. And he liked that too
Despite the British.
"It's all one," he said.
And he died chanting,
"La illa ha il Allah hu!
La illa ha il Allah hu!"

"There is only God."

losing my religion

*Many minds moving have settled on matter
as the crux of the problem. And the problem
does matter, even if, when you reach the end
of the rope, you find yourself thinking never mind.*

*Ramakrishna's Kali's a material
girl in a material world, so coming
to the heart of the matter where he began
is more or less a matter of time for a young man
with a mind to get to the bottom of things,
one way or the other.*

There is no god but god appears to contain something for everyone within earshot of the muezzin chanting. But the matter of and has given many minds moving pause.

"Lovers don't finally meet somewhere, they're in each other all along." Only

there is.

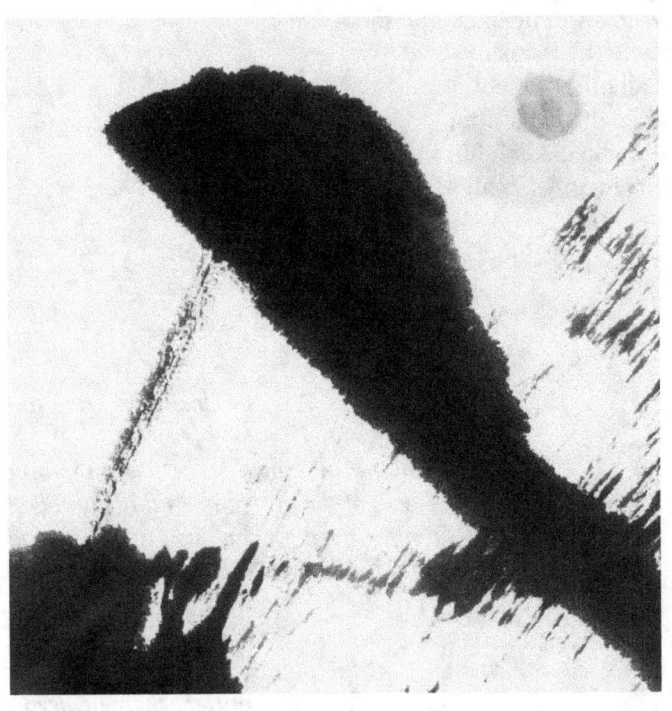

The Rose Led Us to Our Eyes

I suppose
I like it
That I can "like"
Mirza Ghalib
On Facebook.
And
Get the news
That I can join
Him @world-
Chains, a new
Social net-
Work.
Ghalib liked
Friends, after
All. But
Virtual might
Strike him
As bad as
Those
Promised
In paradise—
"It is true
I shall drink
At that dawn
Pure wine
But where
Are the
Long walks
With drunken
Friends?
Where the
Drunken
Crowds
Shouting?
Where

There is
No autumn
Can spring
Exist?"
I like
That.

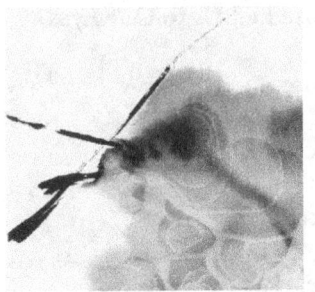

stat rosa pristina nomine...

*Six centuries or more and still
we struggle to discern
the real divinity
in what is present.*

*Ulrich's as if twitters
in every avatar asking
to be friended with
one touch,*

*and you want to say
that takes time
and repetition.*

*Being the friend of a dead poet
on a living network is as
old as the first poet's dying*

*before the second,
and older than proprietary
software that is woven of face*

*time, not philia. Meet the words where
you find them, but never give up
drinking with your friends,
eyes open for roses.*

Gigabytes and Mark 9:21-25

"Where is the wisdom
We have lost in knowledge?"
Eliot asked.
"Where is the knowledge
We have lost in information?"

"How long has this been happening to him?"
Jesus asked a father.

Wisdom.

"From childhood. Often it throws him into fire
And into water, to destroy him.
But if you are able to do anything,
Have pity on us and help us."

Information.

"'If I'm able'!—
All things can be done
For the one who believes."

Wisdom.

"I believe! Help my unbelief!"

Knowledge.

Jesus said,
"You deaf and dumb spirit,
I command you—get out of him
And don't come back!"

Information lost in wisdom.

sola fide

*Elijah's come and gone, and all these people
saying lord lord have no idea what to say
what not to say even when they
see with their eyes and hear
a dark cloud say listen,
this is my boy.*

*It's not hard to believe
the other way the tale is told,
Peter (who knows who he is) saying
we should build a house here now and stay.
Jesus (who names names) calls him
Satan when he stands in the way.*

*Jesus probably has this in mind when he comes
shaking his head and asks what the lawyers
are squabbling about before he turns
to father and son to get to
the bottom of things.*

*Spirits (who know who he is) can't be still
when they see Jesus, and he thinks again
of Peter craving a place to stay
on a holy mountain when this one
takes to dancing in the boy.*

*How long? he asks a second time,
and the father tells a likely story of fire
and water to make an end
that sounds familiar.*

*Get out says Jesus (who names names
and the name this time is what the spirit does)
and don't show your face around here again.*

*The spirit out, the boy looks like a corpse, but Jesus
takes his hand and puts him on his feet again.
Then he goes in and his disciples
still looking for a place to stay
want to know why*

*they couldn't cast it out. Weary,
Jesus says this kind will go nowhere
if not on a wing and a prayer.
Now get out.*

*It was the crowd closing made him name
the demon what it does before it cried out
and he went in. The command and the cry
of a deaf dumb spirit the sign
an unbelieving and perverse*

*generation knows it
cannot live without.*

*Know? No. But
it is possible possible
possible it must be possible.*

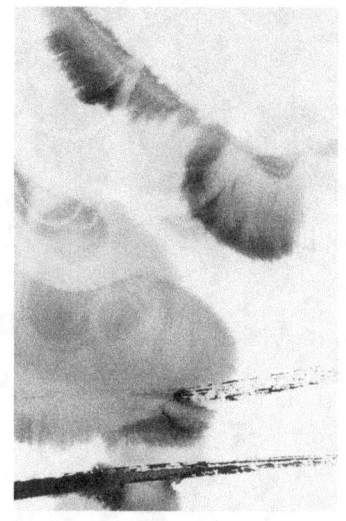

The Tale of an Ass

Balaam got up in the morning,
Saddled his ass, and went to see
The princes of Moab.

Now, God's anger was kindled
Because Balaam was doing this,
And so sent an angel,
Who stood in the way.

Now, the ass saw the angel,
Sword drawn, and so turned,
Going into a field.
Balaam hit the ass.

The angel went a little further on,
Standing on a vineyard path,
Stone walls on each side.
When the ass saw the angel,
She crushed Balaam's foot
Against the wall.
Balaam hit the ass again.

The angel went a little further on,
Waiting in a narrow place where
There could be no turning, right or left.
When the ass saw the angel,
She fell down under Balaam.
Balaam dropped his stick and got his staff
And hit the ass again.

The LORD opened the ass's mouth
And she said to Balaam,
"What have I ever done to you
That you strike me three times?"

Balaam said, "You are mocking me!
If I had a sword, I'd kill you right here!"

The ass said, "Aren't I the one you
Always ride, ever since you got me?
Did I ever do this before?"

"No…" Then the Lord
Opened Balaam's eyes
And he saw the angel
Standing in the way
With sword drawn.

Balaam bowed, falling flat.
The angel said, "Why have you
Hit the ass three times?
Look, I stand here because
You are perverse. The ass
Saw me and saved your life."

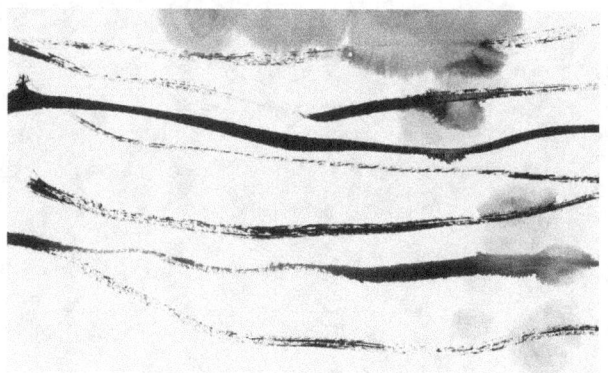

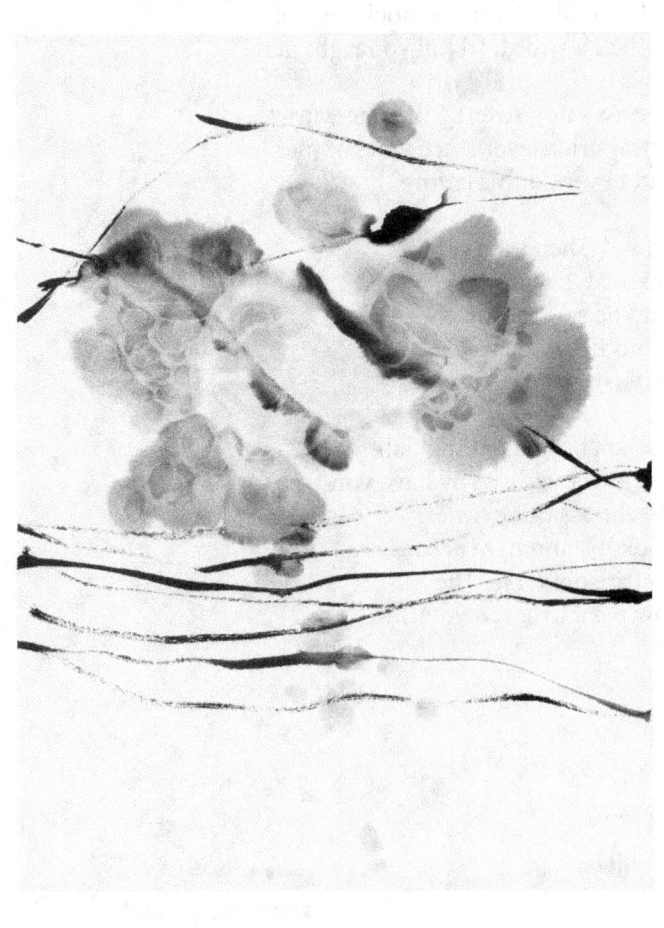

VI

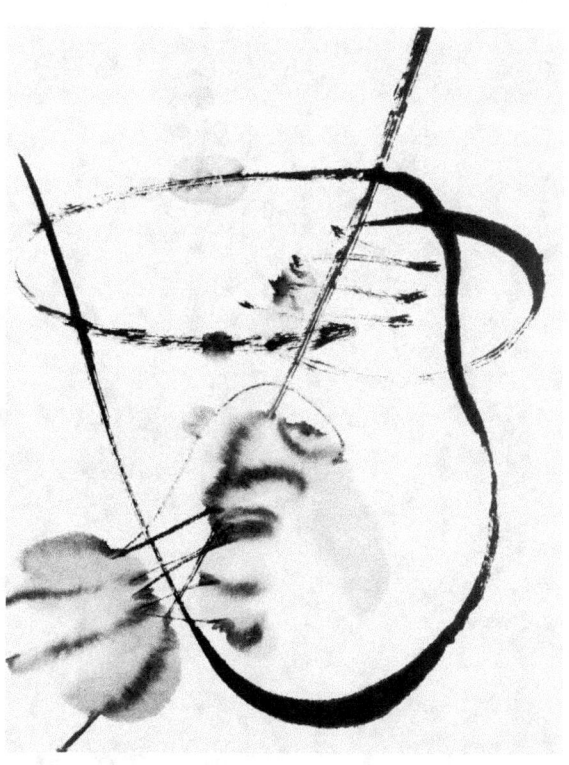

A Note from St. Paul (1 Cornithians 14: 7-10)

it don't mean a thing if it ain't got that swing
—Duke Ellington/Irving Mills

> *Even soulless things that bring sound into*
> *being—say aulos say kithara—how*
> *would you know the sound of aulos*
> *or kithara unmarked as making music?*
> *And if the sound of the trumpet wavers, who*
> *will prepare to go to war? If your tongues produce*
> *no clear signs, who will know what you are saying?*

> *So many sounds in the cosmos, nothing soundless.*
> *But you are talking on thin air until you*
> *lay your hands on soulless things,*
> *breathe a breath of life into them,*
> *give them reason to sing.*

Company B

Who wants to be a pipe
For Fortune's finger
To sound what stop

She please? Hamlet
Does a little dance
To that tune, William

Fingering the notes.
Bugles. Harps. Pipes.
We pay our dime,

We get our dance,
And the dance
Dances us. Just for

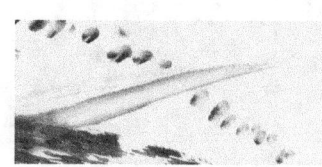

A bit of fun—let's not
Call it illusion—we call
So many things soul-

Less. Subhuman. Ours.

The better to
Eat you with,
My dear.

prophesy

*Still, from where I stand
it makes me want to imagine
a letter back. All those epistles,
some rustic Origen must have been
moved to dictate a reply:*

*Paul, Paul, do you need another bolt of lightning
to get the idea of the soul of the world, a feel
for a geometry of solids that sees soul
in every thing?*

*But even a loose translator has to dance
with the one who brung him, play
with the letter hoping there's spirit
enough to make the congregation
get happy, hope someone catches a glimpse
through a crack and shouts prophesy.*

*Poor Paul never quite got over being
consumed, but he had friends
who opened every letter,
invited him back for another drink,
thanked the lord for whatever
knocked him off his high horse once,
played aulos by ear, never missed a chance
to jam with some old flatland farmer
flat picking an old guitar.*

*Paul just dropped in to see
what condition his condition was
in. Even with no boogie-woogie bugle,
his friends said good, Paul, still very good.*

Beyond, Way Beyond

Paul had to smack
Those Galatians,
And his anger wasn't
A sin (because he
Said so): When you
Did not know God
You worshiped things
That were not gods,
The weak and beggarly
Elements, watching
The seasons and stars.

But now…Galatians,
Get with the Desert
God paradigm, dis-
Embodied. Way above
And way, way beyond.
So far beyond you…

Well, anyway, don't
Get circumcised.

Love, Paul

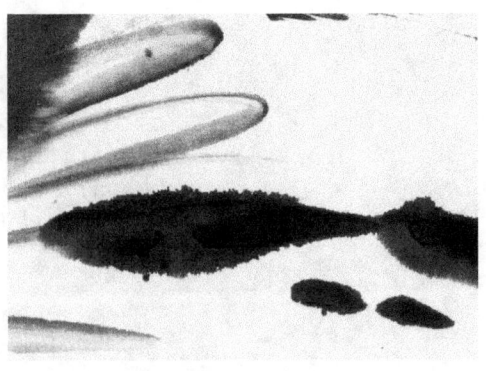

A Spectre Is Haunting Europe

Paul,

*It's all
beyond me.*

*But I know it makes me feel
like dancing, this desert,
when it leaves me*

*empty. Or
the mountain,
where I think this god*

*of yours once
lived, above it all
before he*

*came down to earth
like some shadow
over Miriam,*

*that child who
pondered in her heart
the child who*

*took your sight so
you could see
your breath*

*so you could breathe
and as I live and breathe
you do live and breathe it now,*

and we love you for that. But still
the heavens declare
and empty

the desert sings
the work of god's hands
the way

a voice echoes
on an empty mountain.
There. See?

Love your work,
A friend in Philippi

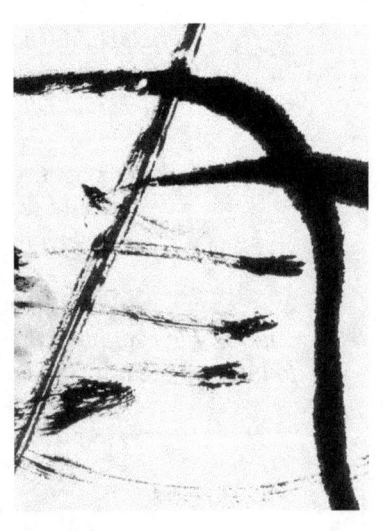

Dear ____,

Titus here.
Paul wanted
Me to drop
You a line.
He says
He thinks
What you think
Is OK but
You need
To talk,
Next time
He's through.

And remember,
Cretans are
Always liars!

Grace, Titus

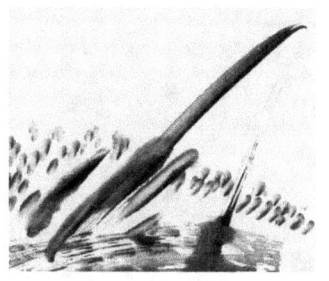

Titus,

*I know you are
a man of your word,
so I am penciling this in as
we speak (so to speak).*

*We'll do lunch. Talk
about old times.*

*Nothing like breaking bread
together and sharing
a bottle of wine*

*to clear up differences.
Have Paul call when he gets in.*

Till next time then.

*Peace,
Waiting on tiptoe in Philippi*

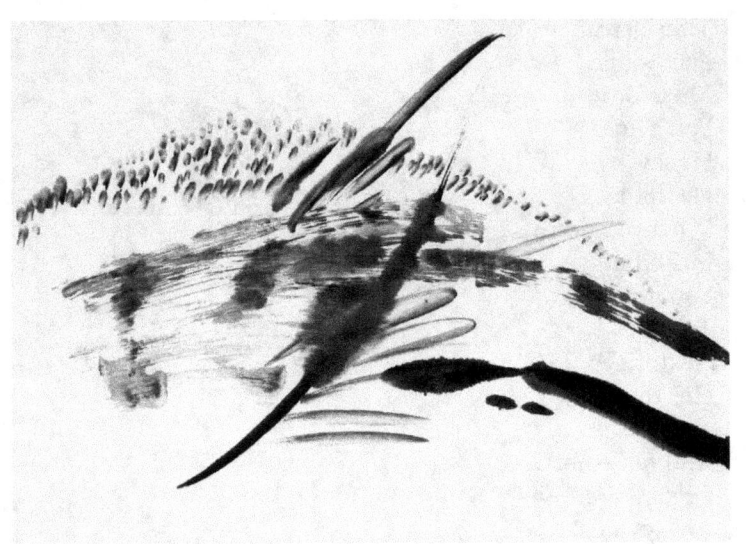

VII

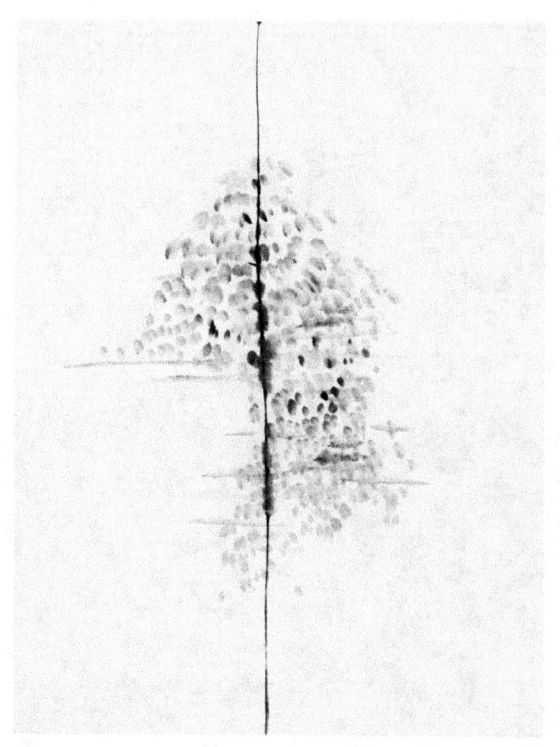

If Only Evil

Oh, if evil only were
Like a black hat that
Could be doffed or
Changed. If evil only
Were like an abscess,
Like a cancer that
Could be lanced or

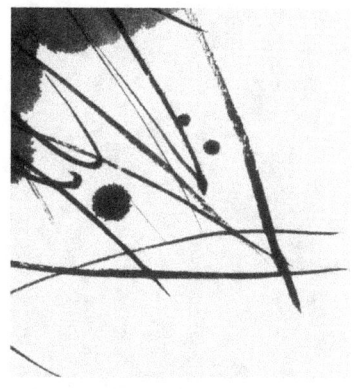

Cut. Could be excised
Or chopped. If only
Evil were only other
People: that one or
Those there. If only
A Satan were behind
It all, plotting; fated.

If only evil
Weren't just
Ourselves
On a bad day
Acting badly
For all the
Right reasons.

one day is as good as

*turning, always
about turning, not
what we do on a bad day*

*for the right reason but reason
spinning on good days
(and one day is
as good as another) until, dazed,*

*the good we would we
do not do*

*the good news is
it's all connected the bad
news is it's all connected all*

*coram deo, nothing
outside when god is said
to have said it is good, nothing*

*outside when god is
said to have said no other
nothing outside when Jesus*

*looked the Rock right in the eye
and said, Satan, get back
someone said*

*language is a virus from outer space
and that might just be what John
had in mind in the beginning*

*word on the street is the beginning is
an act, and that's not all bad,
especially if you turn*

*to god and some old prophet says nothing
doing if you do you will surely die
and you say tell me something*

i don't already know and do

RUAH

Every time I talk with angels
We come to loggerheads when

It comes to logos. Why are they
So bullheaded about a word

Like The Word? It must—
Don't all sounds—say, mean

Something. "Breath," they
Whisper. "It's only breath."

yes

*only take it,
now, all of you,
breathe, yes, do*

Breathing Lessons

I remember one woman
Who took a long time to die.
I'd get called at 2, 3am
That she was hyperventilating
Again. "Can you do anything?"
The nurses would ask. I'd
Listen to the same stories
Because she couldn't remember
Yesterday, though fifty,
Sixty years ago worked fine.
Her alcoholic husband again;

How he beat their son; sexually
Abused their daughter. "How
Could I, how, let that go on?
And now…I'm just dying.
I'm just dying alone now,"
She sobbed, saying how
She regretted it all, sobbing
Until she couldn't take a
Breath. "Try to breathe," I'd say.
"We forget how sometimes.
For now, just try to breathe."

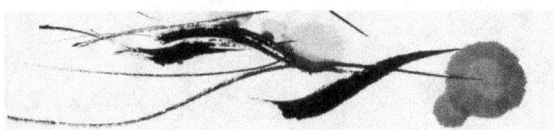

VIII

Undecided

*Paul (if we are to believe
the letter) says to Titus the Cretan
who said all Cretans are liars (meaning,
I assume, Epimenides, who was
a poet, bringing to mind
the claim a friend of mine
who writes fiction once made
that poetry is fiction and writers
of fiction are liars by profession)
was telling the truth.*

*Now, Titus, repeating this, could claim
he was no Cretan—just some goy
Paul abandoned on the island
to get things organized. And
he may have a point.*

*But my question, Zeno,
is whether you can prove
it is not possible to travel from
the poet Epimenides (point A, let us
say) to the mathematician Kurt Gödel (shall
we call him Zed?) by which you might mean to say
there is an unbridgeable gap between poetry
and mathematics. Minding the gap,
I refer you to Scott Buchanan.*

*But Paul himself, I think (or was it Peter?), said
his people were peculiar, which makes them,
I guess, members of an abnormal set (by
which we might mean to say an
ekklesia), like something that is not
square, a member of the set (itself not
square) of all things not square and thus
a member of itself. A body that is a member*

*of itself is either a mystical body or a self-consuming
artifact. What do you make of god consuming
god's body with the whole creation
(or would that be only friends in truth?)
at a big table? I can't decide,*

*but I think Ludwig was on to something
when he said "wovon man nicht sprechen kann,
darüber muss mann schweigen."*

*Having nothing to say, say nothing.
And that, John said, is poetry.*

Zeno's Employment is Not the Case

"Cretans!" Wittgenstein yelled,
As you might too after months
In the trenches. Achilles will beat
The hell out of a tortoise. And
Don't even get me started on
How arrows will get way over
Half-way there. The world is all
That is the case. And let's call
What is the case—what exists—
A fact. And let's say a logical
Picture of facts is a thought—
Stay with me here—and that a
Thought is a proposition with

Sense. We won't be after any
"Ergos" here. Make sense?

Let's just say lying
Cretans are named Titus;
Can you picture that?
Make sense?
Achilles gets there first.
Picture that.
Bullets don't stop to measure.
Zeno isn't employed
By the war department.
We don't have to say any more.

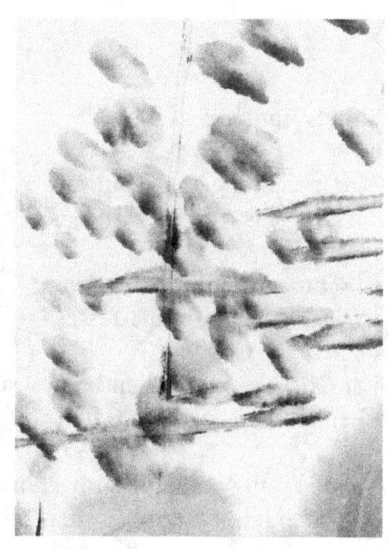

We're All Soldiers Now

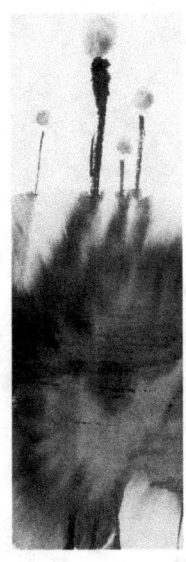

"That," says Paul, "is what
I'm talking about. We
don't have to say,
but let me tell you
a story. An umpire once
said, 'I call them as I
see them.' Another said,
'Well, I call them as they
is.' A third chimed in, 'They ain't
nothing till I call them.' We
don't have to, but we
will."

And that, being the
case, is, so to speak, the world.

Sportsmanship

"Do it. Call me out," Paul says.
"I take pleasure in infirmities,

In reproaches, in necessities,
In persecutions, in distresses,

For Christ's sake! When I am weak,
Then am I strong. Just watch

While I pull you behind my chariot
As I march in triumph someday!"

sting

That's why I believe in Susan Sarandon.
It's all in the delivery, and the chariot
don't mean a thing
if it ain't got that sting.

Where's your victory now?

Whatever Floats Your Chariot

"I'm making myself
as scummy as I can,"
Rimbaud wrote. "Why?
I want to be a poet
and I'm turning myself
into a seer." Yes,
disarrange those senses,
Arthur, until you ride
Your drunken chariot
all the way to modernity.

And it came to pass,
as they went on and talked,
that, behold, there appeared
a chariot of fire,
and horses of fire,
and parted them both asunder;
and Elijah went up
by a whirlwind into heaven.

Quick, Elisha, grab
that scummy mantle.

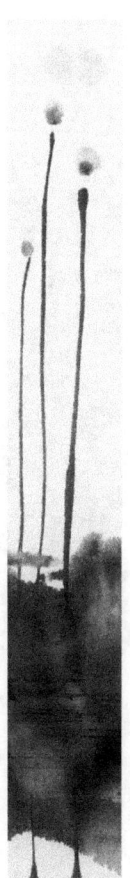

breathe through your eyes

*Growing up in tornado alley, I
learned to keep an eye
on the whirlwind and
a respectful distance,
especially when there was
fire, noise, and anything parting
asunder. Granny would grab us kids
and run for the storm cellar
at the first sight of a tail in a dark
bank of low clouds on a muggy day.
But Grandpa liked to stay
above ground, even
when it touched down,
get in the pickup and do
a little dance with the thing.
"Don't try to outrun it," he'd say,
"just watch until you have an idea which way
it's going next and drive across it." Each saying
"Get out' the way" in their own way. As for the mantle,
Arthur, Elisha, my advice is not to try too hard.
Yankee fans and Okies born and bred
will tell you it's a non-prophet business now.
They'll pay to win, and one way or another
they'll drive you to drink. Keep a chair
waiting at the table, but there
will never be another Mick.*

*If you're a pitcher, don't think,
take it as a gift of grace,
breathe through your eyes,
and keep that flame burning.*

Clarifying Question

Nothing like a tornado
To teach salvation, life's
Questions boiled down
To: How are you gonna
Save your ass now?

My grandpa swore there
Was one sapling on a road
He was walking down one
Day, one solid thing for
A mile to hold to and so
He did, and he got pulled
Head over heels, he swore
Holdin' on for dear life.

Nothing like the green
Light and wind culled
Down to a breath-sucking
Roar to pare the questions
To one: What are you gonna
Do to save your ass?

My aunt said one twister
Plucked all her geese
And laid 'em out gutted
As pretty as you please.
But my uncle I never believed
Who said one came so close
He didn't need to shave
For a week. I'm sure that's
A lie. But I know there's

Nothing like a tornado
To trim things down
To one good question:
What will you do
To save your ass?

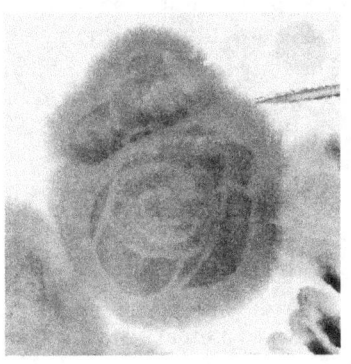

Teshuva,

I understand
In Hebrew
means both
repentance

and forgiveness
tough concepts
to reconcile
like boiling ice

or innocent drinking
where I come from
in the desolately
fertile Midwest

where repentance
is all one way
and forgiveness
all the other and

the last people
we would dream
of forgiving
are ourselves

do a little dance

*as usual, it's nothing
or a stick of compassion*

*folks who remember doing
something to save their asses*

*have almost always forgotten
dumb luck and the grace of god*

*take it as a gift, breathe
through your eyes,*

*set an extra place at the table,
do a little dance with the damn thing*

nothing, like a tornado

*turning, again, turning
again, turning
always*

*to embrace what was
always there,
turning*

*a little dance
and the world is new*

IX

all I know

*the incarnation of a god is evident
in memory out of place.*

*a baby reaches for what used to be
an old man's prayer beads,*

*and believers know
he has come again. but*

*in this body
all I know
is there
is comfort
in believing*

*every child who reaches
for what used to be*

*before her eyes
could be*

*remembering—
like a buddha, living*

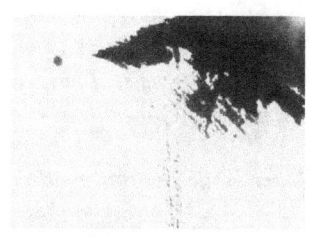

Pantoum on Grasping

Before the horse has left,
The donkey arrives,
Said the old Zen master.
One darn thing, another.

The donkey arrives,
Lingyun said of thought—
One darn thing, another,
The mind won't let go.

Lingyun said of thought—
Look at the images:
The mind won't let go;
We grasp desperately.

Look at the images,
Said the old Zen master—
We grasp desperately
Before the horse has left.

This Bodhisattva is Going Nowhere

Said the old Zen master:
The crowd busy unloading the cart
before the horse has left,
the load grows heavy, the cart empty.

The crowd busy unloading the cart
with one hand, piling on more with the other,
the load grows heavy, the cart empty.
Emptiness, said Qoheleth, is all.

With one hand piling on more, with the other
we pile on less.
Emptiness, said Qoheleth, is all.
Always more or less emptiness to pile on.

We pile on less
before the horse has left,
always more or less emptiness to pile on,
said the old Zen master.

Qoheleth Makes a List

Oh, how we love our obstacles,
Says the Teacher, but this also
Is empty air. Laughter. Mirth.
Wine. Still we thirst for wisdom.
Tears. Depression. Protein
Shakes. Oh, how we hug our
Fences, ditches, walls. Obstacles.

How we drum on things
To disguise the silence.
Makes me wanna be a moralist,
Says the Teacher. Makes me
Want to make a list. Yet that
Too is empty air. When I think
Of races; battles; plans;

When I think of dead lions;
Makes me almost a moralist,
Says the Teacher. Yet the one
Who watches the wind
Does not sow; the one
Who watches the clouds
Does not reap. And the light…

It's sweet. And it is a pleasant
Thing to behold the sun.
Not bad, this empty air.

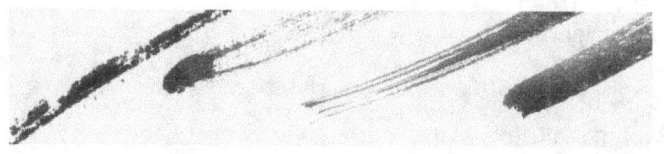

a forgetting of air

> *Circular forms seem suited to sadness,*
> *Preacher—turn turn turn time and time*
> *again, like maple seeds on autumn.*
> *But a touch of spirit on the sadness*
> *in it reminds me it is a step one can dance.*
>
> *There is, Luce says, a forgetting of air*
> *in Heidegger, all earth and fire and water*
> *and blood. Not the emptiness, not*
> *even the cart before the horse, more*
> *or less, the piling on. There are lists and*
> *lists and of the making of moralists there is*
> *no end. But master and preacher have eyes*
> *with something of the sun in them.*
> *See, this empty air is not bad.*

Doing Something: a Round

Why only one song, one speech, one
text at a time?
Luce Irigaray

In his being
And in his time
Martin got
A thing or two right.

When we are born
We are the DNA,
When we die
We are the trace.

Brother Paul, I have been meaning

to tell you how much I enjoyed
those words you said about praying
with mind as well as spirit. I had half a mind
to shout amen right then, but I wasn't quite sure
at that moment I fully grasped the spirit
of what you were saying. I had it in my head
you thought strangers would fall down
at the feet of god (so to speak) if
five intelligible words were spoken
by one person after another in order.
But I can't recall a single instance of a stranger
falling down awe-struck no matter what
anyone said if she hadn't been dancing all night
heart and soul to some music. A place for everything,
I suppose; but I think you might want
to think again about license.

I've been going over it in my mind,
and every time I'm pretty sure
god has spoken, it has been
a shocking thing (I think of all that water-
soaked wood bursting into flame on Carmel).
There's more power in that than you can know—
and that's the good news. You remember that time
you were struck blind on your way to put things in order
so you could see? There might just be something
to see in that about silence—if you see
what I'm saying.

But I think I got the part about chili and the cigarette
on a cold day for a quarter. It's all about heaven
being a matter of timing, right? Right place,
right time. And the more things change,
the more they stay the same.

Two Thoughts on Prophecy (1 Corinthians 14)

1.
Heaven is a cigarette,
The old man said,
Right after a bowl

Of chili on a cold day.
Back then you could get
A bowl for a quarter, but

Everybody was hungry.
I don't know when,
But it'll be that way again.

2.
Speaking in tongues is fine,
Paul said, yet that doesn't
Say anything to anyone but

God. Speaking in tongues
Is good for the self;
But prophecy is good

For the people—teaching,
Comforting. There are,
Paul said, it may be,

So many kinds of voices
In the world,
And none of them

Without meaning.

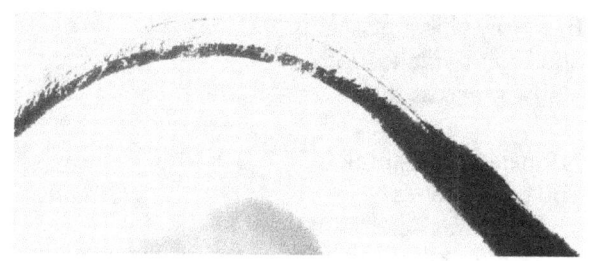

Knocked Right Off Her Horse, Amen?

Now that I'm old enough
To have my own fake tooth
Maybe I'm old enough
To see the wisdom
Of Sister Alma, whose
Favorite prelude was, "After
I met him on that
Damascus Road, I knowed
I was goin'
Where
I didn't need to be!"

To which many would shout,
"Testify, sister! Testify!"

Now she would be called
Pastoral Care Associate.
Then, we called her Sister.

Now she would be called
A cancer survivor.
Then we called her a miracle.

She was hope incarnate,
Maybe especially when,

In a Holy Ghost fit,
She'd spit her fake tooth
Halfway across the church.

"Hopeless? You think
You got hopeless?
My Jesus was dead
As a door nail.
And just
Look
At him now!"

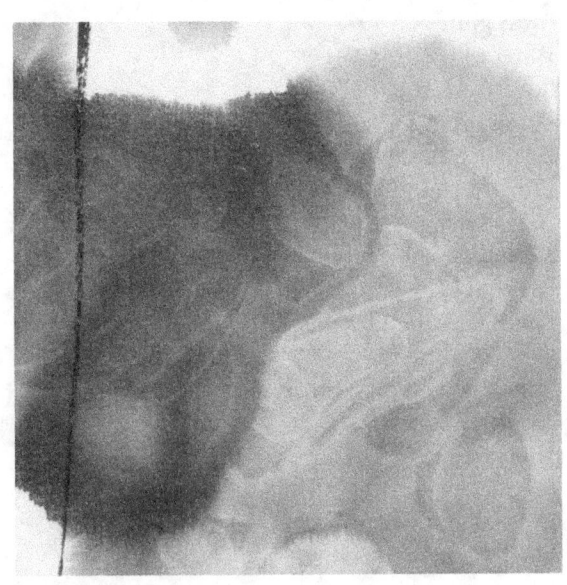

be still

*That's what I'm talkin' about.
Sister spits her fake tooth
halfway across the church,
Paul says "order," and you know
damn well he don't need to go there.
I'd still call her a miracle and say
to Paul, "Jesus, child, be still."
You see what I'm saying?*

Cryptomorphs

No, people
Who have
Never heard
Of Jesus
Can't see
Him in
Their toast.

People who
Don't know
Mary don't
Have her
Showing
Up in
Their pastries.

Imagine that
—Mold, stains,
Tortillas
Without
A chance
At redemption.

apokatastasis

*If you can't taste the miracle
in every tortilla hot off the comal
and the loving hands of a good cook,
it doesn't much matter whose face you see*

*where or when. Guadalupe and Guanyin took Mary in,
but they were there before a word of her was
spoken. Sometimes it seems
redemption is all*

*a misunderstanding, every knee
bowing now at the mispronunciation of one
name or another while the heavens declare not
a chance—it is done.*

What Part of "Stasis" Don't we Understand?

So many flavors
Of personal gods,
Fifty-seven varieties
To say the least.

We want our luck
And we want it
Buttered, the old
Saying goes.

Reconstruction.
Restitution.
Rescue.
Return.

Get me back,
Oh, some god
Or other, get
Me back to that

Primordial condition
My condition was in,

Back before I saw
The hindquarters
Of the universe.

Yes, there's got to be
An Eden, a condition
Before; a use-ta be.
There's gotta be
A genie in a bottle
Sort of god I can
Conjure for

All three
Of my precious
Wishes. Buttered,
If you please.

I'm just saying

*Well, yes, Marduk had almost that many names
all by himself, but no Eden to speak of.
Standing here now, it seems to me*

*it's more about the arc of the universe (if
you will) than a wish for some
primordial condition,*

*the condition our condition is in,
long, but toward justice, all
good, still very good.*

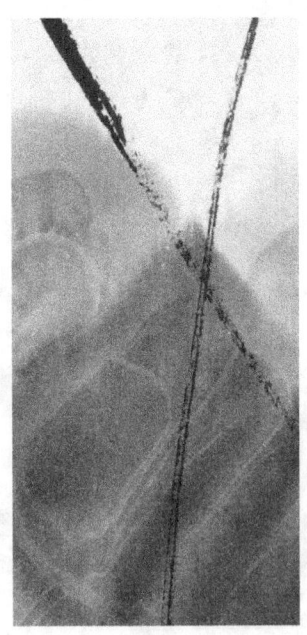

Yes, Children, Marduk Ascendant

Before the sky had a name,
Before the earth had a name,
When the deep that begat Marduk,
And the chaos that was mother of both
Still were a single mass,
Before any land was, even marsh,
Before any god had been named…

Well, yes, we know that story,
Moving over the face and all that,

But Marduk was a practical god,
Rising like any politician—
Sociopathic murder and
General chutzpa—until, well
He had several priests to recite
His several names…

After all, it is the constitution
That matters, cosmology
Doing very little in the way
Of forming ethics, and Marduk,
Well, he liked his laws,
And, bless him, shared
With his buddy Hammurabi.

And the rest is, well, history,
Which sometimes is not myth,
When we read very carefully

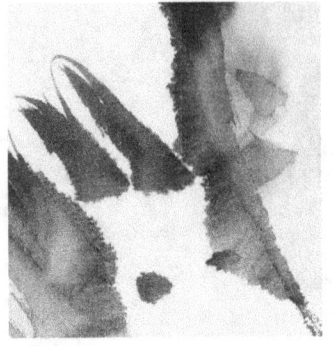

always

Care, yes, always
care. And never confuse
making myth with lying

or simply being
misinformed.

Name names, and always
keep a cosmos in mind, mind
in cosmos as you constitute

a city there. It's all history,
and how we sing it
will always haunt the world.

Those who do not
learn from it, as some
old philosopher is said to have
said, making place of space dwelling on it…

How It Really Happened

Both praise and praiser
Have a short life,
Marcus Aurelius said,

Emperor out on
The German frontier.

Both remembered
And rememberer
Have a short time,

And that only
In a tiny corner
Of the world.

And even there,
Not all agree—no,
Not even one person

With himself.
And this whole earth—
It's only a tiny corner too.

only so much

*No, not one. All
our dwelling is in
one tiny corner or*

*another. Seeing so
little, we say so
much. Only*

*so much. Always
remember.*

Only so much.

List of Awesome Power (There Will Be a Quiz)

These are the kings that reigned in the land of Edom
before there reigned any king
among the children of Israel:

Bela the son of Beor reigned in Edom
and the name of his city was Dinhaba.
And when Bela died
Jobab the son of Zerah out of Bozrah
reigned in his stead.
When Jobab was dead
Husham of the land of The Temanites
reigned in his stead.
And after the defeat of Husam,
Hadad the son of Bedad,
who defeated the Midianites
in the field of the Moabites
reigned in his stead
and the name of his city was Avith.

When Hadad was dead
Samlah of Masteka reigned in his stead.
When Samlah was dead
Shaul of the river Rehoboth reigned in his stead.
When Shaul was dead
Baal-hanan the son of Achbor reigned in his stead.
And after the death of Baal-hanan the son of Achbor
Hadad reigned in his stead
and the name of his city was Pau,
And his wife's name was Mehetabel,
the daughter of Matred
the daughter of Mezahab.
Then there was Dwight Eisenhower.
And such are the rulers of the earth.

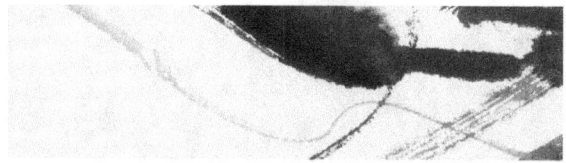

awesome

    and after ike mehitabel
    hooks up with archy
    a hunt and peck
    poet of necessity
    made like ike's roads
    to survive nuclear war
    and hang with cats who
    used to be big time but have
    had a chance to forget so much
    and always had their hearts
    in the right alley toujours
    gai kid toujours gai
    let the people say
    toujours gai

mehitabel at the key

leapin key
2 key is
one ting
wotsgot
easier wit
time

no click
nottin
moves

but dem
liddle
lectrons

light on your feet

Easy's gettin' harder every day
—Iris Dement

> i know you were at one time
> cleopatra, mehitabel, and you
> must have been pretty damn light
> on your feet to survive in politics
> as long as you did,
>
> but every time my cat lands
> feet first on a keyboard,
> something has to give,
> and it's not her rolling in
> silent soft and gentle

*like a fog. today, they say
neutrinos fired at Italy
from Geneva arrived
early, and i have some
inkling why she's always*

*out of sync. she's spent her
whole life taking waves collapsing
when some nosy physicist opens a box
personally, but she could always be sure
nothing travels faster than light.*

*now this, and she may
have to rethink the whole
universe. small wonder archy
dumped the old underwood long ago for a
mac with voice recognition and a mic built in.*

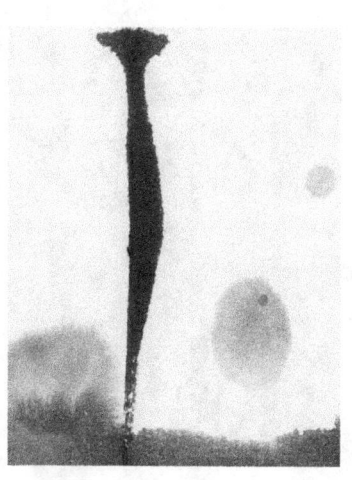

Buddhism and Schrödinger's Cat: Just Think About It

No, Subhuti,
Wisdom cannot be learned
or distinguished
or thought about
or found through the senses.

Forget thinking about it;
Forget about naming
this and that;
only experience teaches.

Yes, Schrödinger,
your cat is screwed
(pardon the expression)
well before any atoms decay
merely in having
an owner like yourself.

There is a difference,
Schrödinger said, between
a shaky or out-of-focus
photograph and a snapshot
of clouds and fog banks.

He knew this
because he
had been there.

No, Subhuti,
you can't
have a cat.

Litter-Bearing

There's a reason
There are no cats
In the Bible—

Sleeping as they
Do like bridesmaids,
Like servants, like

Thieves in the night.
Worse than
Balaam's ass for

Backtalk. Oh, yes,
With attitude like
That who would

Need a Satan
To step on
Job's keyboard?

Sure, mice are
A plague. But
For sheer bad

Similes cats
Would bear
Away the litter.

yes

*yes, no
cat can be
had, and that*

*is that.
light can be
wave or particle*

*but it cannot travel
faster than a cat
collapses*

*when she has
her mind on sleeping,
without a second thought*

deus absconditus

Cats know how to lay low,
so where there is no
word but a shadow,
a cat is in the corner
of some eye, taking it in.

The Bible is full of shadows
where nothing is said,
and there are cats
there to turn
the tip of an ear
when god says where
were you when—under the radar,
every one a deus absconditus between lines.

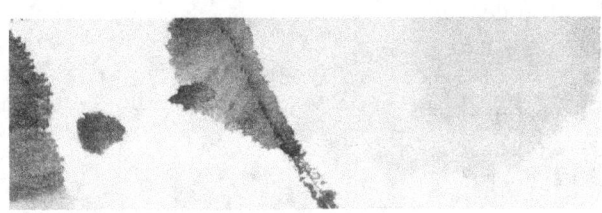

Party Line, Ezekiel 16:6

Both my grammas were healers,
One Cherokee, the other Christian.
You don't even want to know
What the Cherokee one said, but

The Christian one wouldn't take no money,
No, not for the gift God gave her. And
I understand as soon as she got a phone,
The crank type, an oak box, people started

Calling her up. They'd call her bleeding, for
Her only gift was to stop the bleeding.
A chopped off toe; a hand in the thresher;
Childbirth; gun shots; that sort of thing.

What she did was quote Ezekiel 16:6,
The new phone medium faster than
A horse, yet still magical somehow,
But only on certain tongues, like hers,

And when they called she knew the words,
"And when I passed by thee,
I saw thee polluted in thine
Own blood. I said unto thee,

When thou wast in thy blood,
Yea, I said unto thee, When
Thou wast in thy blood, Live.

That's all it took.
Party line Clo
313. Call anytime.

de profundis, call

for what we do not want to know
for sons and daughters
sacrificed

we have heaped up riches
and our arrogance
has grown

we think we think
the thoughts
of gods

mark iniquities and who
shall stand? throw
that load down

new heart, new
spirit, no
desire
now

that is all

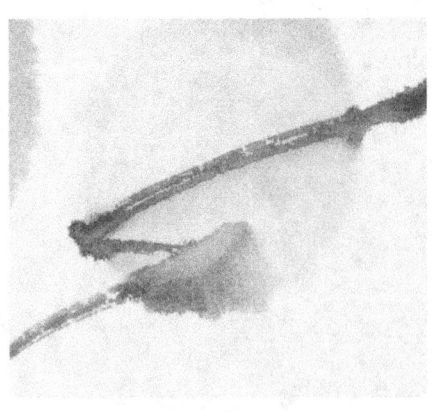

Jesus Does Some Writing

At least he didn't have to
Worry about glass houses,
But when they asked about
Killing people, the rabbi
Who would get the 'ol

Capital heave-ho himself
Took a pause to write
In the dirt. How to honor
Old laws without busting
The spirit of the new?

Let the one
Without sin
Do the killing.

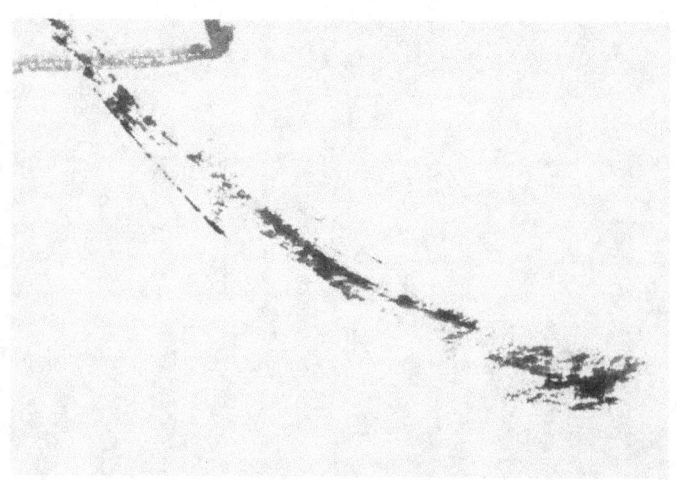

X

Thought of, Thank You

Paul of Samosata
Got a bad rap
For thinking through
Just where Jesus
Got his divinity.
Not denying a
Thing: just thinking.

All that had
Already been
Thought of, thank
You, explained the
Top brass—"Here's
The answer, thanks,

"And, if you don't
Keep quiet, well,
Let's just talk about
All those women
You might have
Slept with. Let's
Discuss some money
It may be you took."

Paul stuck to his story
And got not "saint"
In front of his
Name. so—was it
Just the ego
Of one more
Protestant?
Is it, after all,
Truth we're
After or
Certainty?

likely stories

*Truth be told, I think we're looking
for likely stories—or (more likely) stories
we like—to settle on more often than not. Once
we settle, possession is nine tenths of the law,
and nobody wants to think about moving.*

*Never give where god settles a second thought
if you have your heart set on sainthood.*

*A saint is nothing but a zero
to keep a story in line,
and a protestant in any given
time and place is nothing but a pain
in the ass the powers that be
have in mind when they happen
to be naming names.*

*The question is not god but what we mean
by we, and the secret to sainthood is not being there
then, out of mind out of sight waiting on
the right story at the right time.*

*Nothing is more unsettling when
you're trying to get your story straight
than a person thinking about god
settling with friends you don't know.*

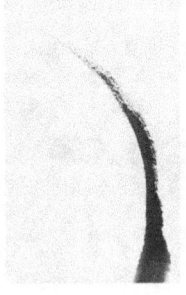

For Good of the World

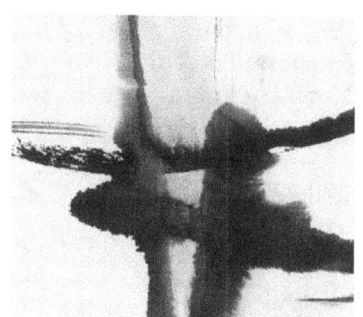

Site and situation—
Every religious act
Is a political one:
Obeisance, rebellion,
A claim for reality.

I wandered at
A monastery once
From cell to cell
Where nuns had
Been bricked
Into the walls,
A tiny slot for
Letting the food
In, waste out.
No light, no
Sound but their
Own and…God?

Yes, they knew
Where their
Prayers went.

I wandered from
One to the next,
All the same—so
Many lives given
To…God? To
Order, coherence?

A site where
Randomness could
Not intrude and
The eternal only
Mattered? Every
Religious act is
A political one.

Obeisance;
Rebellion.
Was that
What they
Thought?

shekinah

what is at stake in every act is
the city we will
inhabit where we will

see walls the side we will
call this the side we will
call that who we will

call in who we will
call out when who we are
at war with of necessity who

we will make saints to contain who we will
declare insane which prisons will contain
us others to some other we who made them

out of mind out of sight on every other
side what matters makes its way
like a river to where it was

before we got our stories
straight before it was
contained in them

a maker of scenes
every step we step we step
on holy ground we cannot take it in

No Shekinah on Wall Street

Who really wants
Revolution in the streets
When there's good TV
And a warm bed at home?
Yet the years gone;
And the wars going on
And on; yet starvation
And silence in the face
Of endless need.

The Talmud says
The Shekinah
Never did come down,
Nor did Moses
Nor Elijah go up,
For the Psalm says,
The heaven,
Even the heavens,
Are the Lord's
But the earth hath he given
To the children of men.

No one wants
To camp in the streets;
Yet wars and starvation;
Yet murder and no
Justice; yet a generation
Lost. The earth hath
He given to the children
Of men but businesses
Have taken it away.

With justice the cobblestones
Stay in the streets;
With justice children stay home

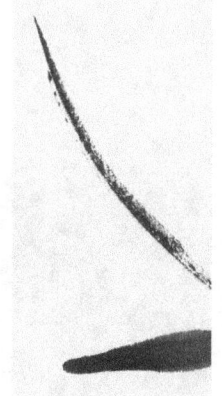

To live their lives. But that
Is not now. The earth that
He gave to the children of men
Has been taken away.

Tenting

*When you get right down to it, shekinah
has always been a small letter scene
on the make. Nobody owns nothing,
and no body means no place*

*where a divine presence dwells. Gil
wrote that song before the revolution
was a twenty-four hour news cycle
dedicated to the proposition
that no news is good news,
and programmers know now
as well as then that will
keep people on or off the street
where they can keep an eye on them.*

*Wars and rumors of wars are business
as usual, bad things made by men
and children of men and the question
remains what kind of scene
the children will make their image,
what kind of god their image will make at home.*

The Deep to Pomegranates

Some tents last a good long while,
Like the Tabernacle that sat at Shiloh
Three-hundred-sixty nine years. And not
Even nylon, for all that. If only the LORD
Had invented Eddie Bauer a bit earlier
What might have happened in the world?

Yet so much was already lost
When the Israelites stopped pulling up
Stakes and hitting
The desert on a whim.

It was enough to make a poor angel cry
When the wandering ceased. It was,
Angels knew, only a matter of time
'Til some darned king or other took to
Comparing tits to pomegranates.

Ah, the wind gone out of the sails,
As it were, of the religious mind.
Where was the mighty breath
Blowing over the deep in all that?
Oh, the revenge of the concrete.
Enough to make angels cry.

Oh, humanity;
Let them settle
And they just
Settle and settle.

the long art of concrete

I won't deny the material
has a good deal to do
with how long the scene
lasts before you take it down

and move to settle on some
other place. Life is short, but
the long art of concrete
might make you think a city

could go on and on. But a good
long time is not too long, just
long enough, and one typhoon
is all it takes to unsettle settling

there, king or no. I imagine
pomegranates a balm for heartache,
and things that move angels
to tears leave eyes clear.

Take a deep breath, and you will
know the wind still broods over
the face of formless deep,

restless, looking for some adam
to unsettle with another breath of life.

Jobs! Jobs!

People said one to another,
"Come on, let us make brick
And burn it with fire."
So they used brick
As their stone
And slime as their mortar
And they got down to
The muddy business of
Building a city, day to day.

And the tower went up
And expectations rose
And every foot it rose
The tower became more
Important than the people.

And soon the only cry
Was "jobs! Jobs!" and
All the people knew
Was firing up bricks
To use as their stone
And mixing more slime
To use as mortar.
The muddy business
Of business day to day.

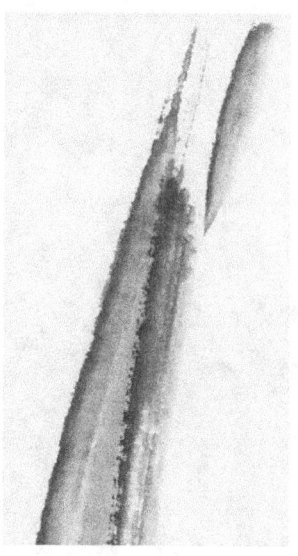

One day YHWH came down
To see the city and tower.
YHWH said, "See
The people are one
With a common tongue.
Now that they have begun
To do this they
Will not leave off
Until the only cry

Will be 'jobs! Jobs!'
Come on, let us
Mangle their tongue
So that one will not know
What another says."

And it was so.
For a while.

come on down

*That Babel story has had me
scratching my head for years.
Far be it from me
to second guess
a god. No doubt gods
have access to intelligence
we can't read, but this one
seems a wee bit insecure.
And a person in power who fears
the power of the people speaking
with a common tongue seems
human, all too human.
YHWH did come down,
you say. Some say, by the way,
that descriptions of his intelligence agency
were based on the Persian secret service,
and we all know what that meant
for Job. Are you sure that wasn't what
they were all worked up about?
But here's the thing.*

*A city that is all business
seems to me all wrong.
Building a stairway to heaven
may be a pipe dream,
but it sounds like fun.
And I've never known good
brick layers to need much
in the way of a common tongue
to get a job done. Just sling the mud,
put the bricks where they belong,
and smooth the mortar so
anyone who lays eyes on it can see
this was a job well done.
What's to talk about? You'd think
YHWH of all people would appreciate
a beautiful thing made with spirit
and mud. Let the heavens declare—and
come on down for the music
when a good day's work is done.*

Plumb True

It may well be
That the LORD
Got faulty intel
On weapons of
Mass destruction—

Babel's tower
Wasn't a slam
Dunk like
Gomorra
And Sodom.

Blame it on
The Babylonians
Who catch it for
Everything from
Introducing angels
To their captive
Hebrew audience

To that night and
Day thinking
That brings
The Great Satan
Into the picture

Let alone eternal
Punishment and
Whatever the other
Is.

I never have caught
The method of
Using a plumb line
To get a wall true

Or laying bricks with
Level in one hand
And trowel in the other.

It never struck me
As leaving a hand
For the bricks.

I admit I
Often miss
The obvious, but
At least the LORD
Can rest assured
My walls won't
Ever be a threat.

XI

every one is a world

a heretic is just some dumb schmuck
who made a choice once, and if
you don't know how many
lines pass through
each one

Heresy!

ask Hugh Everett, who will tell you
What to do with those   *every one is a world with a snake*
Who choose for themselves?   *in it, and you can't imagine*
What to do,   *bling enough to fill them.*
What to do
With those with
Consciences they
Choose to listen to?

Oh, my, the implications
Of thinking for yourself!
Heresy, heresy,
Thinking for yourself.

And what to do
With heretics?
What to do?
Just pitch me
In the trash
When I'm gone,

Hugh Everett said.
It's all one.
Pitch me
In the trash
When I'm gone.

Oh, the
Implications!

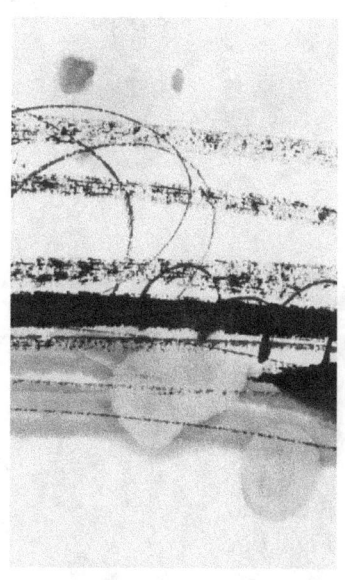

one way or another

*I think Hugh said anything that can
happen will happen. And it does
happen. And it is*

*happening. And
if it's all the same to Hugh,
I take that to mean the possibilities
are limitless. Not*

*to decide is to decide
may have become
the stuff of Hallmark card
slogans and cheap print posters
that come with the plastic frames
you buy in Walmart to keep
them from putting
emptiness on display.*

*But Jean-Paul was on to something.
Everyone does, and one way
or another we all hang
in the end.*

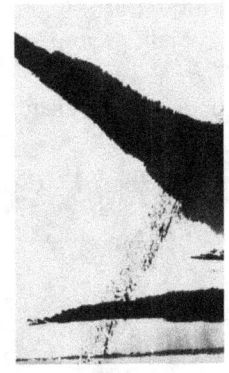

To Decide is To

Huineng taught
That wrong ideas
Keep us from
Enlightenment

But so do
Right ones.

Huineng, the master
Who taught that
Sudden enlightenment
Could be very, very

Sudden.

But, Master Huineng,
Wrong and right
Be damned, we
Still have to chose

The burger or
The tofu. We still
Have to chew

The humble pie
Of decisions that
Maybe it is
The universe

Swallows whole but
Feel like a bone in
The throat of little

Me.

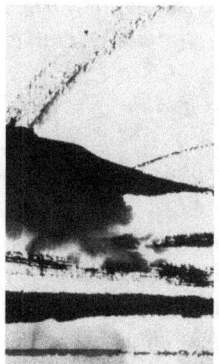

> **no**
>
> *liuzu was no*
> *ascetic, but how*
> *could li matou*
> *know*
>
> *him*
> *otherwise*
> *in his sangha?*
>
> *no tree*
> *no mirror*
> *no self*
> *no dust*
> *to settle.*
>
> *no bone*
> *to pick*
> *no swallow*
> *no sudden*
> *all at once*
> *bird's eye*
> *no idea*
> *now, no*

By "You" I Mean Me

The mind is pure;
You've really got to
Work to mess it up;

The way is easy;
You really have to
Try to make it hard;

But just look at you:
You've managed to
Muck it up. Look.

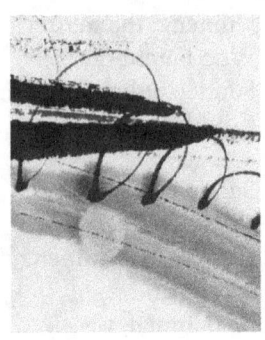

By "We" I Mean I

*No doubt. Filthy rags and all
that. But we do love to complicate
things. Where's the challenge in
a way with no hairpin turns?*

*We're all children who can
never resist stirring up
a mud puddle, jumping into
the muck, eyes on elsewhere*

*hoping for something to splash
around in, taking the corner
too fast to prove we are still alive.*

*Good thing Jesus had his eyes open
when he said his city is a city of children
(who can never abide plain and simple).*

*Good thing Gautama knows
how to laugh. Good thing Guanyin
is going nowhere with compassion, fast.
Good thing the world is still mud-luscious in spring.*

My Advice: Jump in a Puddle

"I just watched my aunt;
I just watched my mother
Just waste away…to

…Nothing," she says.
"I know what it looks like
And I've just got, what,
Twenty years myself?
What's to hope?" She says,
"Don't gimme afterlife,
I'm wasting away now.
What the hell can I do
Another twenty years?"

And when his followers
Said to Jesus, "When
Will you appear to us?"

He said, "When you strip
Yourselves naked
Without being ashamed,
And you take your clothes
And dance on them like
Children, then you will
See me and not be afraid."

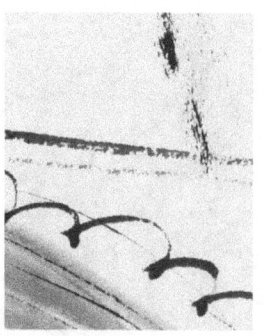

let the people say amen

*We always have all the time in the world
in every moment we have, and a theory
that muddies the water with an infinity
of possible worlds is one hell of a puddle
to jump in. Play on, and let the people say "amen."*

XII

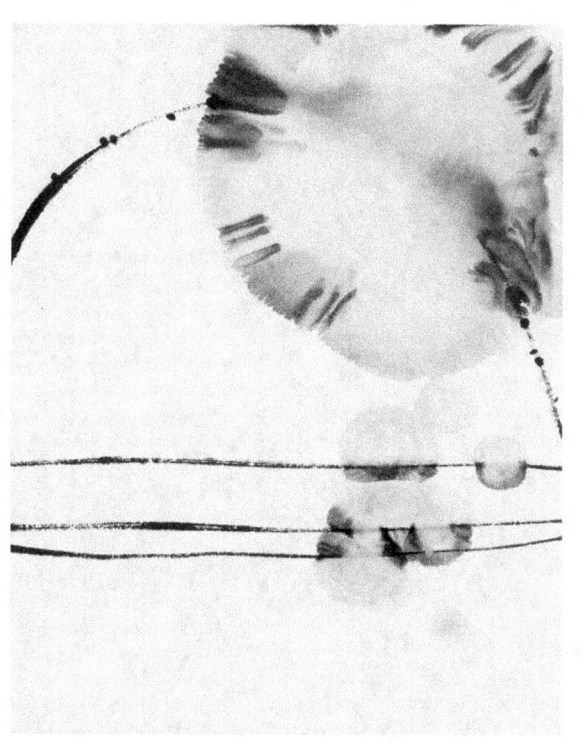

do this in remembrance

on the other side of the river a guy moving north
    fast against tourists and the light says as
        he passes when i walking south stop
            either are you on *or* do you want
              cocaine? *and there is no time
                  to say* come again? *and
                      even if i knew*

    which, i would have nothing to say but wonder
        as i often do what makes him think as i
            listen to the sax player who is

        playing as he often does on mondays when i
            pass this way and sway a little
                to the music as the light
                    turns and i turn

            and the music fades in no time. still
                  music makes me
                      wonder

absent but for memory as it does, as i do, often.

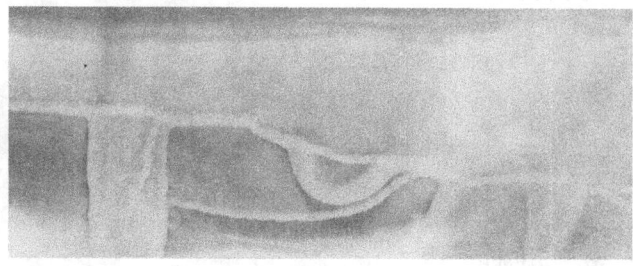

Three Views Out Death's Window

1.
When I was young
I took a Greyhound
Through the delta
Of Mississippi, red
Clay roads wandering
Off into thick pines.
"Look out that way,
Son," an old man,
Drunk or demented
Or both, said once,
Pointing off into one
Of those paths. "Down
That way just about
A mile—you can get
Anything ya want. An'
I do mean anything
At all." "Good to know,"
I said, going back to
My *London Review
Of Books*. "Not bleedin'
Likely," I thought with
The temerity of youth.

2.
"At the end he was
himself again," his
Mother tells me as I
Struggle to eulogize
A man plagued by
Delusion, but only
Age sixteen to fifty-
Three. Otherwise
—He was himself.

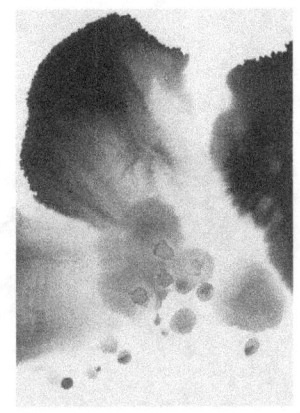

1

thinking follows thing
thought—first
thought second—
best thought after the fact
the fact is no
thinking with no
thing to follow
the thing is one
thing follows another
without a second thought

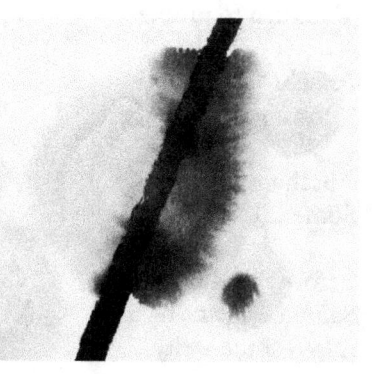

2

Time and History

One damn thing
After another
Damn thing, that's
History, Churchill,
As in Winston, said,

And time, one damn
Thing after another
Damn thing, all
In a queue
To be named—

Damned thing one,
Damned thing two,
And another, get
In line, damn
Things, queue up.

3

but what do you do
about breaking the queue?
there's always someone (i
think it was Ward who
said this) who thinks he knows
the end, so he muscles in
to get there first, and when
the chickens come home
to roost, he gets all bent
out of shape about following
orders. That's the party line—
red flags everywhere, for us
or against us and one
damn thing after another
until all hell, American
as cherry pie, breaks loose

4

And ain't it the flags
That turn to problems

Anachronisms of
Time and tribe

Abraham cooking up
Some calf with butter

Before the law
Said no, for strangers
Off to smite a city

For God knows why
Wrong flag, one assumes

And a god before he
Got fed up with milk
Mixed with his beef
A god who could say,
Go ahead, Sara, laugh
But you're knocked up

Bake your cake and let
Angels do the killing

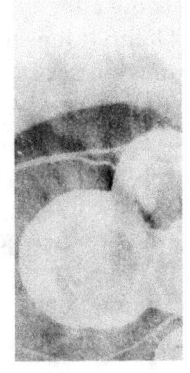

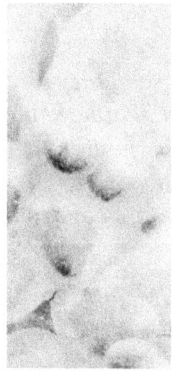

5

*Even the people's flag
is a problem, even
when Billy Bragg
brings a tear to my eye
singing it. Deepest red is
the color of blood, and you
don't need Leviticus
to know that's an abomination,
even if it's the girl next door
who's shedding it. Sarah laughed
to keep from crying, and I
suppose that's why
Miguel said we have to learn
to spill out into the streets
and weep. Otherwise
we'll think ourselves angels
and die laughing.*

6

Fencing the land
The Diggers taught
And owning it came
By murder, plunder

The power of sword
And law is about
Passing on the evil
To children's children

Who have forgot
What it is they stole
The Diggers taught
Until that is

They got killed in
Their unfenced Eden

7

The old, they said
cannot kill the young
forever, dig?
Dig, and diggers
are not dead.

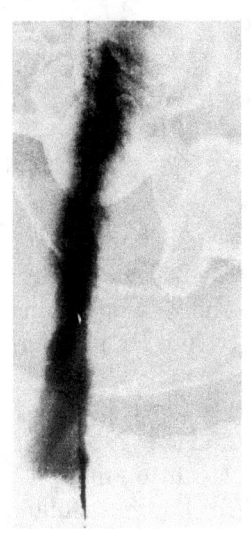

8

A friend sends me
My family tree, tracking
Exponential boxes
Back into old names,

Benjamin, Abraham,
Effie and Evangeline
Two boxes, four,
Back and back the

Dead line up to get me
Here, in their sweet
Obscure ways, the dead,
Illiterate, silent, a row

I tick off, reading back
Who are they, this
Line of quiet names
Gone to soil every one

9

About the past,
I am at present
of two minds.
It is a heavy thing.
Every tenth cousin
weighs the wait
of the world.
While I am dying
to move it, it moves
as it has moved
as it will move
when it does
move, at its own pace.
But a cloud of witnesses is
in it, and they call
my name. I
name them one
by one and there is
a world I know
where the god who makes it
goes one story higher, sees
flowers in graveyards, sees
it is good, it is very good.

10

In the year 2525
I sang, when it was
A hit, the song

Nineteen Sixty-Nine
The numbers growing
And human life

Disappearing as
The numbers grew
3535, 4545

"If man is still alive"
And that didn't sound
So very likely, being

Around, with war
And space and drugs
My mind on the infinite

To a little pop ditty
In the year 2525
I did the math

It didn't look good

11

Not bad to a cockroach
with the soul of a poet
and a cat who was Cleopatra.
A poet with the soul of a cockroach
might get that song
out of his head
and land on his feet
playing the numbers. No man
is an island, and they say
cockroaches will survive us.
I keep an old Underwood
in the closet
so there will be free
verse when we are gone.

12

Is that what I do?
Is that how I do it?
Why are the letters
All out of order?

I wondered nearly aloud,
Biting my lip
To the rhythm
The teacher made,
Flexing her wrists just so,

This is how to hold
Your wrists, she said;

Whack, whack,
Whack staccato
Of metal on paper.

Home row, home row,
She twittered
So cheery I wanted to slap her.

Boys don't need to type,
Not touch typing,
She'd said. But you can try.

And the words, words,
Quick brown foxes;
Return your carriage!
Letters and aching wrists.

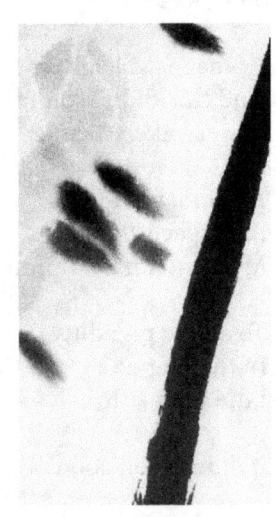

13

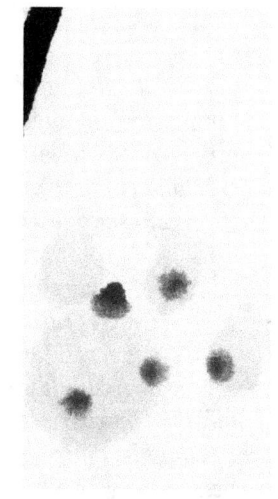

getting letters in order
is like herding cats
slow
but possible
if you learn to want them
to go where they are going
everybody needs touch
typing, every letter
needs the whole
weight of a body
to move it, every word
more than the sum of its parts
twittering quick brown foxes
staccato makes a whole
body ache
if you have something to say
and are no bigger than
the plane surface
of one key
in a word
machine

14

On the train I tap out
Letters on my phone
As sensical as
Words on wires
Pink clouds at sunset
After a day of snow
Somewhere
In the plastic
We've wrapped
Round ourselves
There's blood still
Raging for the exit

15

*blood raging
in plastic language
makes words wireless
cloud computing
sunset, moon
not far
wine still
makes tipsy
poets reach for
it, drown atwitter
plucking blackberries
when they could be dancing
shoeless on holy ground*

16

Where's the tipping point
Privilege to right
Favor to expectation?

Job had his reasons
For bringing up some
Baggage he had...

Kohelet, though
Preacher, pedant
Isn't he beyond

The pale

Calling all the racing
On being
Nothing new

Same burned omelet
Different millennium
Nothing new

Under this sun

17

*Job had reason
on his side. That is why
his crazy god could do nothing
but shout non-sequiturs
when they stood
face to face.
Where were you when is
no answer to now
what is this
all about? Kohelet
has a point. Every river
flows into the sea, and the sea
does not overflow. Hard to see,
though, how that follows
from emptiness.
The softest thing in the universe
overcomes what is hard.
If everything is wrong,
it is because nothing makes it work.*

18

We are but filthy rags!
he shouts in the street,
poor beings who know
nothing. I want to say

Oh, that's Isaiah
something isn't it?
but he's not the sort
to be asking that

not his trope
the distinctions
no, i think it's our
righteousness that's

rags, I want to say
not us, whatever we
be. It's our superiority
in the street that's

filthy and raggy

19

*whatever it is
we're trying
to clean
gets worse
with every swipe
we take at it
if we knew nothing,
we'd have nothing
to say and sigh,
one step short of
a song and a dance,
a poem where mind goes*

20

I missed the part—
I must have been
out of the room—
when someone said

don't think about it.

I missed the part—
was I staring out
some window?—
when someone said

That's no beezwax

of yours, you know.
I must have been
dreaming somehow
when the news came—

Don't bother

21

*Don't you worry your pretty little head
is a phrase I'd over
heard more times than I can count
by the time I strolled off more or less
at ease into the belly of the beast
for a higher education because
accidents of birth meant
it was never meant
for me.
I had seen the best minds of my generation
wasted by straightjackets woven as often as not
by snake oil salesmen in pulpits
repeating that bullshit from the whirlwind
as if they were in it, without a doubt
that they had the power
to make everything right.
The power behind them is hard
to deny, but I've known enough tornadoes
up close and personal to know anyone who is in one
is out of control. All that shouting is a sign
that the right is another matter,
and the wasted minds
set me to thinking
about thinking,
something it seemed
preachers and other politicians
didn't much think about.
Thinking about thinking makes you act
slow, stutterstep, gives you time
to see the poem where mind goes,
through word to sigh, through
sigh to song, through
song to dance.*

And when your body moves, you know
where mind begins. You turn
then, embrace a world
that has been dying to be born.
No question we think, I think. The question is
how to think like a poem set free on the world.
And don't that make you wanna dance?

22

time and chance it seems
happened to them all
just as the preacher said
time and chance the cutting edge
time and chance the broken window

how make it say?
always the gauntlet
chance and time throws down
time and chance
how make it say?

the rest is vanity
always to the swift
time and chance
the rest is vexation
how make the poem say?

time and chance it seems
happeneth to the them all
just as the preacher said
the rest is—how make it
say?—vexation of spirit

23

time and chance
dance poems
where mind goes,
sing. listen
for sadness in
cold wind, listen
for the music of a red
leaf breaking a cobblestone
line, listen to Spring shattering
barbaric glass, listen to the shadow
of every blackbird
time and chance
cut both ways
blood cries
out from the ground
it says, listen

24

Snow piles in its silent way
While I read Jeremiah, angry
About cakes baked for the Queen of Heaven

What was it God did with his wife?
Why was it the prophet got so angry

Over cakes of crescents, cakes of stars
And a little wine on the side,
A few snacks baked for the Queen of Heaven?

What was it God did with his wife
So terrible it could not be spoken of,
Could not even be possible she had
Ever existed at all? What's so bad
About some Moon Pies for the Queen of Heaven?

The divorce must have been one lulu
To drive her all the way back to Egypt

The snow is up to the bottom of the chairs
A cold blanket over a few old words, the only
Crumbs left of cakes for the Queen of Heaven

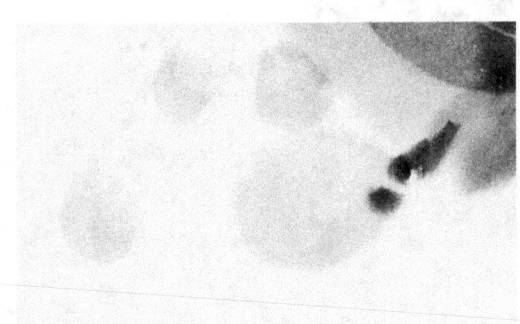

25

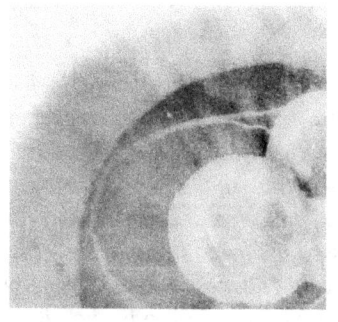

*Snow's silence says
more than any jealous
god can know. This
is Bast's year.
Any prophet worth his salt
knows love divided is
not love
diminished, wine
makes de brighter,
and god knows we
need friends
who can see
in this darkness.*

26

The noises in the basement
May be rats, may be ghosts,
May be some friends I have
Forgotten about. Why check
Speculating? Perhaps they are
Hanging new curtains for
The show stopper, blockbuster
At the edge of the mind.

It's all one, from where I sit.

Later, there may be some
Things I have to do, like laundry,
Shopping, and dying. For now
I say to some other of myself,
Take a memo: All is well. Even
The noises in the basement.
May be friends, may be ghosts,
May be rats. May be curtains.

27

*They say when Luther—startled
by something rustling in a dark corner
out of sight while he worked late one
night—threw that inkwell at Satan,
he was not afraid, because it never
crossed his mind it might be a rat.
Ghoulies and ghosties and long-leggedy
beasties and things that go bump in the night,
a question, I suppose, of what plagues us
here, now, and what we have at hand
to fend it off. Friends, ghosts, rats
it may be now, but it will be curtains soon
enough. And I see no reason to ruin
Old Scratch's Armani over that.*

28

Astarte, Ishtar,
Aphrodite
Queen of Heaven
Gal in the Ground

Why was it your
Guy in the Sky
Got so out of hand?
First the demands

Then out for cigarettes
And you believing
For the longest time
He'd changed, changed

And at every noise
Astarte, Isis,
Venus, Mary
You thought

It was him getting
Over himself
Why was it your guy
Got so into sky

He filled the void
With only himself?

29

*For god's sake, Martin,
you've read Job.
Better to throw dice
than ink while you calculate
the odds of winning at craps
against card sharks like Lucifer
and his spaced out friend.
False shuffles, false cuts, culling,
stacking, a poker face all mean nothing
if you don't play poker with them. Take the odds
and the house advantage is not even
one percent. But you have to be
patient to win at a game
like this. Nothing changes,
and that is that.
You thought Kohelet
was depressed when
all he was doing
was writing
a memo re what happens
when the light comes on
and you see nothing.*

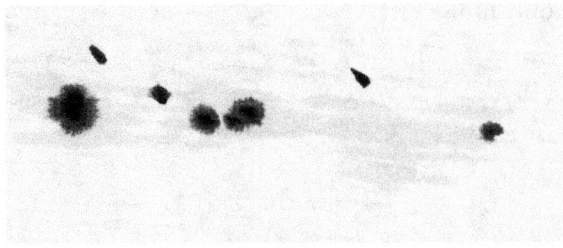

30

When the three sat down
Abraham, Martin, Job
The chips on the shoulder
Matched the chips at hand

And there were still hard feelings
About not asking that Mecca guy

Job brought the beer
Martin got the chips
Abraham was late because
He'd taken his son somewhere

When the three set down
The rules of the evening

There were chips on
Every shoulder, every hand
And in three bowls
Which meant nothing

I'm still feeling bad
About the Mecca guy

Father Abraham said
I smell a rat said Martin
That's justice for you Job said
To no one in particular

31

*I'm thinking the party
back home with
Astarte, Isis,
Ishtar, Venus,
Aphrodite, Mary,
and probably Katie
was the place
to be. No
dice,
better wine,
and the only whirlwind
a passing dust devil when
they clicked their tongues
over the absence of Khadijah.*

32

the patriarchs
and the mommies
the newly wed
and the nearly dead
gathered as they are
in the trailer parks
of memory and desire
where heavy snow
crushes the tin roofs
and everyone says
that's OK, as long
as a tornado don't hit
the matriarchs
and the daddies
gathered after work
to see what beer
is on sale this week
ten bucks for a twelve

can't beat that
Lot says but he
always says something

like that or don't look back
that's the other thing
he says to the daddies
and the mommies
newly wed and nearly
immortal. Don't turn
around for nothin

33

*Eurydice would be
the first to tell you
it's not the turning
the old man objects to,
else Orpheus would have been
a pillar of salt a long time ago.
I don't know how many times
Lot's wife tried to tell him
any man with a temper
like that is bad news.
And she had her doubts
about that Abraham,
slinking off tight-lipped
with his boy. And the look
in that child's eyes when they
came home from the mountains,
not a word between them.
He never could remember
the first boy's name,
and that ain't right.
So what if something might
be gaining? It might be
someone you need
to say goodbye to.
And that old man's son, the one
he always said was the only—
didn't he come waltzing in
late shouting "turn"?
They really ought to make up their minds.
But I'm only human. I figure that means*

*a hell of a lot of turning before
I get it right. And I'll be damned
if I'm going to traipse off without
so much as a fare-thee-well*

*when I leave my friends,
even the ones that get
a little carried away
when they're on the sauce.
Too much spirit and we all
get crazy. You can't
damn a man for that.*

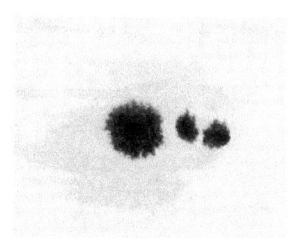

34

The radio said
You can find yourself
Without looking
For yourself which
May be true since

After all Oedipus
Went looking for self
Not knowing it was
Him he was looking
For, the guilty party

That had the plagues
Raining down but
This may not be true
Of cases other than
Oedipal, Orpheus

For example, who
Had a fine time
Strumming until
Other factors called
Him to the depths

35

Was that at the low end of the dial,
where npr and the evangelicals
used to hover uncomfortably close
before they went commercial
and found themselves some lebensraum?
It seems so nearly Buddhist if not
for the assumption that there is
a self to be found. If there is,
rest assured you will find it
only when you are not looking.
Something will surprise you then,
perhaps a plump ripe lychee
in your lap, and you won't know
if you found it or it found you. Either way,
finding is the first act, so you might as well
go ahead and get ready for the second, loss.
And if you've promised to punish the culprit
the moment you find him,
you might just have to turn
and put your eyes out so you can see.

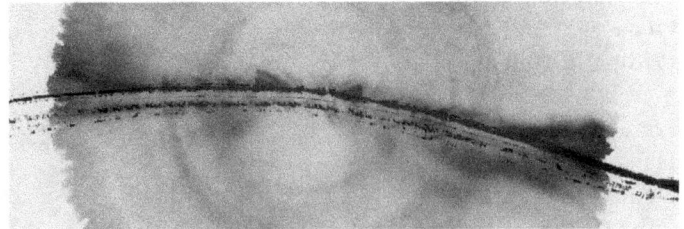

36

I'm not sure why but
I met him sitting beside
his dead ostrich. Not

That I'm questioning
meeting him, nor
why he was sitting

It was just the dead
ostrich part I question
I've never mourned an

ostrich, but I don't
question that either
It's just the part about

Pointing to its wrung
neck I question
Why is it he thought

that a good idea?
Check your Christian
history—it's a symbol

of faith, symbol
of contemplation

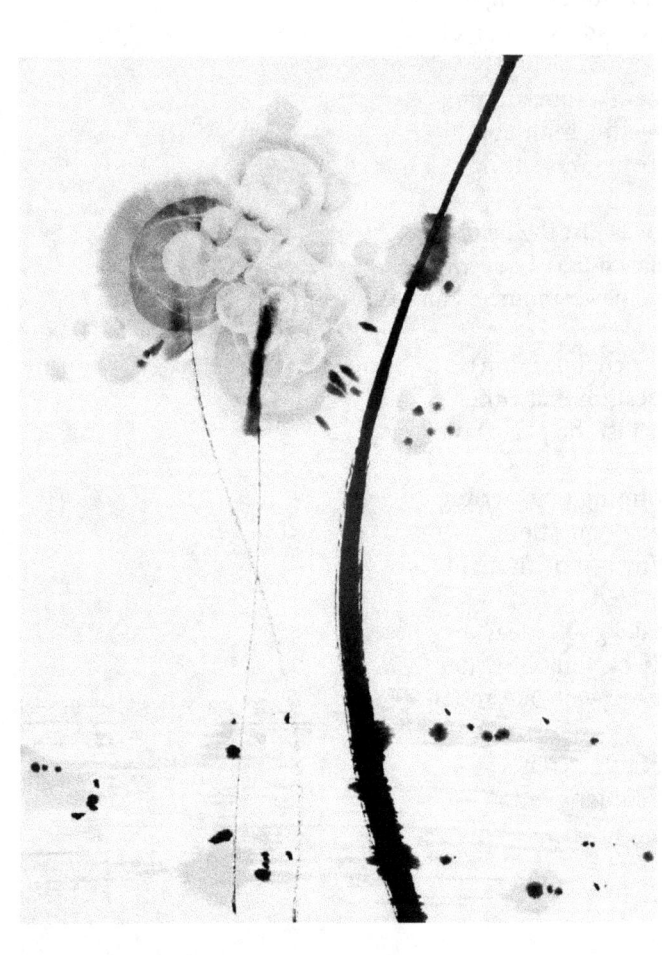

A note to readers on sources:

¶ We have quoted and paraphrased freely from memory, as we do in conversation. To alter citations to make them conform to an authoritative written text would do violence to the poems, so we have left them as they are, leaving it to readers to challenge, correct, question, and locate. The engagement is part of the process we hope to incite with this collaboration.

¶ By way of locating this work in an ongoing conversation, the brief introduction acknowledges our debt to Theodor Adorno, Clifford Geertz, Karl Marx, Paul Ricoeur (and Shenzhen University philosopher Zhao Dongming's reading of Ricoeur), Michael Taussig, and Amos Wilder. Equally clear in the poems themselves will be our debt to Terry Allen, Laurie Anderson, Walter Benjamin, Scott Buchanan, Bull Durham, William S. Burroughs, John Cage, Stanley Cavell, Leonard Cohen, Gilles Deleuze, Iris Dement, Bob Dylan, Empedocles, Hugh Everett, Kurt Gödel, Butch Hancock, Stanley Hauerwas, Martin Heidegger, Heraclitus, Huineng, Luce Irigaray, Laozi, Li Bai, Martin Luther, Don Marquis (or, more accurately, his characters archy and mehitabel), Philipp Melanchthon, Wallace Stevens, Henry David Thoreau, Alfred North Whitehead, Ludwig Wittgenstein, Zhuangzi, and a host of other mystics, philosophers, poets, songwriters, and fellow travelers. The list of references at the end of this note (suggestive, not exhaustive) points to specific sources.

¶ We happily include all the annotations and sources our readers add in the extended body of this book (which, to follow Wittgenstein's lead, is a two volume work including what we have written and what we have not), a conversation that, like every conversation, is out of hand as long as it is living.

¶ The book is open. Come on in.

Adorno, Theodor, "Music, Language, and Composition," in *Essays on Music*. Selected, with Introduction, Commentary, and Notes by Richard Leppert. New translations by Susan Gillespie. Berkeley: University of California Press, 2002.

Benjamin, Walter. *Illuminations*. Edited by Hannah Arendt. Translated by Harry Zohn. New York: Schocken, 1969. [The essays collected in this volume were written in German between 1923 and 1940.]

Geertz, Clifford, "Thick Description: Toward an Interpretive Theory of Culture," in *The Interpretation of Cultures*. New York: Basic Books, 1973.

Ricoeur, Paul. *The Rule of Metaphor: Multidisciplinary Studies of the Creation of Meaning in Language*. Translated by Robert Czerny with Kathleen McLaughlin and John Costello, SJ. The University of Toronto Press, 1977.

Taussig, Michael. *Mimesis and Alterity: A Particular History of the Senses*. New York: Routledge, 1993.

Wilder, Amos N. *Theopoetic: Theology and the Religious Imagination*. Philadelphia: Fortress, 1976.